Probation & Parole
in Practice

Reid Montgomery, Jr. · Steven Dillingham

Pilgrimage
A Division Of Anderson Publishing Co.
Cincinnati, Ohio

CJ Criminal Justice Studies

PROBATION AND PAROLE IN PRACTICE

ISBN: 0-932930-61-1

To the many dedicated probation and parole professionals.

ACKNOWLEDGEMENTS

The authors would like to acknowledge those individuals who assisted in the completion of this text. Our gratitude is extended to Dr. William J. Mathias, Jr., Dean of the College of Criminal Justice of the University of South Carolina for his encouragement and support of the project. The authors are very appreciative of the time, assistance, and information provided by the United State Federal Probation Office (in Columbia, S.C.) and the South Carolina Department of Parole and Community Corrections. Special thanks is given to Ms. Alice Rhyne for her gracious typing support and to Mrs. Beth Mathias for her untiring editorial and word processing assistance. Finally, the authors wish to recognize Dr. Michael Braswell for his endorsement of this undertaking and his professional direction of its completion.

CONTENTS

PREFACE

The first edition of <u>Probation and Parole in Practice</u> is designed to provide the reader with an overview and description of probation and parole systems, and to assist the reader in developing the skills for applying professional knowledge and current concepts in practice. The text is organized to provide coverage of the topics considered most important in understanding the proper functions and dynamics of probation and parole. Historical and descriptive information is detailed to acquaint the reader with the past and present concerns of the profession. The text is unique in that it demonstrates many of the actual responsibilities of probation and parole officers, and allows the reader to test his/her skills through the use of hypothetical cases and exercises. A careful reading and serious approach to the completion of the assigned tasks should provide the reader with a broader insight and more accurate appraisal of modern probation and parole operations.

Chapter 1

INTRODUCTION:
MODERN PROBATION AND PAROLE IN PERSPECTIVE

LEARNING OBJECTIVES

* Recognize the need for probation and parole within the American criminal justice system.

* Explain probation and parole in theory and practice.

* Identify professional and ethical standards governing probation and parole systems.

DISCUSSION QUESTIONS

1. Is there a need for continued and expanded utilization of probation and parole options? Why?

2. What is probation? Explain its dynamics.

3. What is parole? Explain its dynamics.

4. What standards govern probation and parole practices?

IMPORTANT TERMS

Probation	Rehabilitation
Parole	Incapacitation
Retribution	Deterrence

INCARCERATION: A LIMITED OPTION

"Lock'em up and throw away the key" is the view some Americans have of defendants involved in the criminal justice system. This simplistic philosophy of justice, however, does little to relieve the criminal justice system of its many problems. As most students and practitioners of the system (including law enforcement, corrections, the judiciary, and particularly probation and parole authorities) soon realize, the limitations of this approach are substantial.

Today, some of the most critical problems impacting the criminal justice system involve overcrowding and other inhumane conditions of American prisons. Nationally, the prison system is virtually exploding with a current population in excess of 400,000 inmates (U.S. News & World Report, 1982). Research has demonstrated these deleterious conditions to be a major source of inmate dissatisfaction (Wenk & Moos,1972; Montgomery, 1974; Moos, 1975) and even prison riots (Fox, 1972; Dillingham & Montgomery, 1982). In addition to the human costs of incarcerating ever-increasing numbers of offenders in prisons designed for far fewer occupants, the monetary costs alone are staggering. Researchers estimate the average cost of housing an inmate in the United States to be at least $10,000 per year, excluding the capital expenditures for each bed space (U.S. News & World Report, 1982).

When attention is directed to those being processed through the criminal justice system, it soon becomes apparent that not all defendants or offenders pose a danger to the community. Indeed, a sizeable percentage are found to be nonviolent and/or amenable to alternative programs. Since the 1840's when John Augustus instituted the first recognized probation program, the concept of probation has gained acceptance as an essential component of the American criminal justice system. In 1970, nearly 25,000 persons were engaged in probation and parole careers nationally (Report On Corrections, 1973). Currently, there are more than 1.2 million state and federal probationers in the United States (Department of Justice, 1982).

A second option to imprisonment is that of parole, a process which permits inmates to avoid continued incarceration by obtaining early conditional releases. In 1982 the number of state and federal parolees in the United States reached approximately 224,000 persons

(Department of Justice, 1982). The states of Texas and New York led the nation in numbers of parolees with 21,662 and 19,865 respectively.

Having capsulized some of the primary problems faced by the correctional system and having briefly outlined the advent and expansion of probation and parole alternatives, the question might be posed whether or not a strong rationale exists for placing increased emphasis on incarceration as a primary technique of punishment. Besides the previously mentioned limitations, incarceration as an exclusive remedy would seem most improbable in light of society's indecisiveness regarding the goals and justification for punishment. Traditionally, punishment has been justified on the basis of at least four fundamental rationales: (1) retribution; (2) deterrence; (3) incapacitation; and (4) rehabilitation. "Retribution," one of the oldest morality based theories of punishment, generally serves a purpose of revenge or "just deserts." The theory of "deterrence" aims to prevent future criminal conduct, both individually (specific deterrence) and at large (general deterrence). "Incapacitation" requires restraint of persons through isolation from society in an effort to render them incapable of performing criminal acts for a defined period of time. Finally, "rehabilitation" involves the reformation or treatment of individuals engaged in criminal activities with the aim to effect improvement in their behavior. For this reason rehabilitation is sometimes not considered to be a form of punishment at all, but rather a therapeutic process.

It is this final mode of treatment with which probation and parole operations are most commonly associated--although the other theories may, to some extent, prove applicable in certain instances. Despite continuing high crime rates and recent emphasis on retibutive trends in punishment (e.g., death penalty cases), a 1982 national public opinion poll revealed that the majority of Americans continue to favor rehabilitation over punishment by a wide margin (Gallup Report, 1982). As the organization and substance of this text indicates, most probation and parole systems continue the pursuit of this goal--even during an era of tightening resources, changing intergovernmental relations and, of course, continuing crime and public apprehension.

WHAT IS PROBATION?

The word probation comes from the latin word
probatio, which means approval or testing. The first
person to coin the word "probation," which refers to its
current utilization as a technique for suspending an
offender's sentence and granting the individual freedom
during good behavior and under professional supervision,
was John Augustus (Dressler, 1969).

Scope of Probation

Probation as practiced today, is far more
encompassing than it was during its early history.
Currently, probation is used in a number of contexts,
including that of a disposition, a status, a system, and
a process (National Council on Crime and Delinquency,
1972). When the court suspends an offender's sentence
and places the individual under conditions of supervision
and conditional freedom, the term probation is viewed as
a disposition. The defendant may, for example, be given
a five year term of probation, during which he or she
enjoys a legal status somewhere between that of a
confined inmate and a totally free citizen. In this
instance, the probationer may consider probation as a
status, due to the limited rights and special duties to
which he or she is subjected. Probation may also refer
to a system which administers probation services. In
this sense, probation (whether state, local, or federal)
is an organization dedicated to the delivery of specific
services, and is commonly considered a subsystem of the
broader system of corrections or even the entire criminal
justice system. Finally, probation may refer to the
process encompassing a variety of activities involved in
its administration, including investigatory and
supervisory practices.

Elements of Probation

A recent author (Carney, 1977) has identified the
following elements in probation practices:

1. A suspension of sentence, resulting in

2. Conditional liberty, under

3. Professional supervision, subject to

4. Improved conditions, with a provision for

5. Revocation for serious breach of the conditions.

Based upon these elements, the following description of probation emerges:

> Probation is a judicially imposed disposition which suspends the imposition of an original sentence by permitting the defendant to be conditionally released under the supervision of a designated governmental agency vested with the authority to revoke the privilege upon serious violation of the probation conditions.

Applying Probation

Generally, the defendant who is placed on probation is a first-time offender who is not before the court for a serious and/or violent offense. A judge usually considers background information related to the defendant and his or her criminal behavior from a Presentence Investigation (PSI) report for purposes of determining whether a period of incarceration is needed. If probation is granted, a probation plan is generally devised for the offender, delineating his or her duties and responsibilities. Arrangements are made for insuring a proper level of supervision for the client and counseling and/or treatment programs are frequently instituted. While on probation, the offender is constantly aware that should he or she intentionally fail to comply with the conditions of probation, a revocation hearing may be instituted which can result in the reinstitution of a term of incarceration. As a result, probation incorporates a "carrot and stick" approach to reintegration into the community: the incentive is provided and the leverage is maintained.

WHAT IS PAROLE?

When comparing parole to probation, important similarities and differences are to be noted. Both probation and parole require supervision of their clients within the community. Similarly, the techniques of treatment utilized by parole and probation officers are generally indistinguishable. Due to these basic similarities, the two functions are typically combined under one agency and officers are often assigned both responsibilities. Among the differences between probation and parole are those related to the prior criminal records of the offenders and the problems encountered in reintegrating the individuals into society. Parolees usually have more extensive and/or serious criminal records. In addition, parolees experience a more difficult social readjustment process because of their institutionalization and status as an "ex-con."

Parole Defined

The word parole is of French origin and was first used in the context of its present meaning by Dr. S. G. Howe of Boston in 1846 in his correspondence to the Prison Association of New York (Carney, 1977). The literal translation of the French expression referred to words of honor, and were originally used in instances where captured soldiers pledged not to take up arms against their captors. In 1939, the Attorney General's Survey of Release Procedures provided a definition of parole that remains applicable today. The report defined parole as the "release of an offender from a penal or correctional institution, after he (or she) has served a portion of his (or her) sentence, under the continued custody of the state and under conditions that permit his (or her) reincarceration in the event of misbehavior" (U.S. Department of Justice, 1939:4-5).

Elements of Parole

In examining parole in operation, numerous key elements deserve emphasis. Author Louis P. Carney (1977:257) identifies the elements as follows:

1. conditional release,

2. under supervision,

3. with social reintegration the agency objective, and

4. revocation the ultimate penalty.

A working definition of parole can be stated as follows:

Parole refers to the privilege of completing a criminal sentence outside an institutional setting, in accordance with conditions imposed by the governing authority, typically a parole board.

The American Correctional Association (1966:114) agrees that parole serves the following two basic functions:

1. provision of supervision and control to reduce the likelihood of criminal acts while the offender is serving his sentence in the community (the "surveillance" function), and

2. provision of assistance and services to the parolees, so that noncriminal behavior becomes possible (the "helping" function).

Parole in Practice

Generally the inmate who is placed on parole is someone the paroling authority feels can succeed in the community. The Model Penal Code (1962) proposed that an inmate be released on parole when he or she is eligible unless one of these conditions existed:

1. There is a substantial indication that he or she will not conform to conditions of parole.

2. His/her release at that time would depreciate the seriousness of the crime or promote disrespect for the law.

3. His/her release would have substantially adverse effects on institutional discipline.

4. His/her continued correctional treatment, medical care, or vocational or other training in the institution will substantially enhance his/her capacity to lead a law abiding life when released at a later date.

PROBATION AND PAROLE GUIDELINES

Probation and parole operations, like many other professional endeavors, have guidelines and professional standards to which its personnel and clients are held accountable. These guidelines and standards are in addition to the given constraints imposed by law. Frequently these guidelines are incorporated within the codes of ethics of professional associations, within the policy standards of agencies and, finally, within the professional practices adhered to by persons in the field. Examples of guidelines from each of these sources are found in the probation and parole setting.

Correctional Standards

Since probation and parole are sometimes considered subsystems of the broader correctional system, reference to the code of ethics of the American Correctional Association provides some guidance for those associated with this component of the criminal justice system. The American Correctional Association (1981) adopted the Code of Ethics in August, 1975 at the 105th Congress of the American Correctional Asociation. This Code establishes a very high ethical standard of conduct for its members by incorporating professional goals (see Table 1).

TABLE 1

CODE OF ETHICS
AMERICAN CORRECTIONAL ASSOCIATION

The American Correctional Association expects of its members unfailing honesty, respect for the dignity and individuality of human beings, and a commitment to professional and compassionate service. To this end we subscribe to the following principles.

Relationships with clients/colleagues/other professions/the public--
* Members will respect and protect the civil and legal rights of all clients.
* Members will serve each case with appropriate concern for the client's welfare and with no purpose of personal gain.
* Relationships with colleagues will be of such character as to promote mutual respect within the profession and improvement of its quality of service.
* Statements critical of colleagues or their agencies will be made only as these are verifiable and constructive in purpose.
* Members will respect the importance of all elements of the criminal justice system and cultivate a professional cooperation with each segment.
* Subject to the client's rights of privacy, members will respect the public's right to know, and will share information with the public with openness and candor.
* Members will respect and protect the right of the public to be safeguarded from criminal activity.

TABLE 1 (continued)

Professional conduct/practices--

* No member will use his official position to secure privileges or advantages for himself.
* No member will act in his official capacity in any matter in which he has personal interest that could in the least degree impair his objectivity.
* No member will use his official position to promote any partisan political purposes.
* No member will accept any gift or favor of a nature to imply an obligation that is inconsistent with the free and objective exercise of his professional responsibilities.
* In any public statement members will clearly distinguish between those that are personal views and those that are statements and positions on behalf of an agency.
* Each member will be diligent in his responsibility to record and make available for review any and all case information which could contribute to sound decisions affecting a client or the public safety.
* Each member will report without reservation any corrupt or unethical behavior which could affect either a client or the integrity of the organization.
* Members will not discriminate against any client, employee or prospective employee on the basis of race, sex, creed or national origin.
* Each member will maintain the integrity of private information; he will neither seek personal data beyond that needed to perform his responsibilities, nor reveal case information to anyone not having proper professional use for such.
* Any member who is responsible for agency personnel actions will make all appointments, promotions or dismissals only on the basis of merit and not in furtherance of partisan political interests.

Probation and Parole Officer Ethics

In addition to the comprehensive guidelines dealing with corrections, more specific ethical codes are designed for probation and parole functions. One such code is that of the Federal Probation Officer's Association. The code was adopted on September 12, 1960 (see Table 2).

10

TABLE 2

CODE OF ETHICS
FEDERAL PROBATION OFFICER'S ASSOCIATION

As a Federal Probation Officer, I am dedicated to rendering professional service to the courts, the parole authorities, and the community at large in effecting the social adjustment of the offender.

I will conduct my personal life with decorum, will neither accept nor grant favors in connections with my office, and will put loyalty to moral principles above personal considerations.

I will uphold the law with dignity and with complete awareness of the prestige and stature of the judicial system of which I am a part.

I will be ever cognizant of my responsibility to the community which I serve.

I will strive to be objective in the performance of my duties; respect the inalienable rights of all persons; appreciate the inherent worth of the individual, and hold inviolate those confidences which can be reposed in me.

I will cooperate with my fellow workers and related agencies and will continually attempt to improve my professional standards through the seeking of knowledge and understanding.

I recognize my office as a symbol of public faith and I accept it as a public trust to be held as long as I am true to the ethics of the Federal Probation Service. I will constantly strive to achieve these objectives and ideals, dedicating myself to my chosen profession.

Client Responsibilities

Probation and parole agencies have established their own standards and guidelines for their clients. These standards and guidelines provide direction for agency personnel in performing their duties. In one state the conditions of probation (see Table 3), for example, are part of the responsibility of the Parole and Community Corrections Board.

TABLE 3

CONDITIONS OF PROBATION (IN S. C.)

The South Carolina Parole and Community Corrections Board is charged with the responsibility of supervising those offenders who have received a sentence of probation. These offenders, it is believed, can derive the greatest benefit from this noninstitutional program.

The following are conditions for probation:

1. Refrain from the violation of any State, Federal or Municipal Laws.

2. Refrain from associating with any person who has a criminal record.

3. Refrain from the unlawful use of intoxicants and you will not frequent places where intoxicants are sold unlawfully.

4. Refrain from the unlawful use of narcotic drugs and you will not frequent places where drugs are sold, dispensed or used unlawfully.

5. Refrain from having in your possession firearms or other weapons.

6. Work diligently at a lawful occupation.

7. Remain within the state of South Carolina unless permitted to leave by your supervising probation agent.

8. Agree to waive extradition from any state of the United States.

9. Follow the advice and instructions of the probation agent.

10. Permit the probation agent to visit your home, place of employment or elsewhere at any time.

11. Report to the probation agent as directed.

12. Pay all fines as ordered by the court.

13. In accordance with the Appropriation Act of 1980, as passed by the General Assembly, I shall pay a supervision fee of $120.00 per year.

12

Officer and Agency Requirements

The American Correctional Association (ACA), in the book <u>Standards for Adult Probation and Parole Field Services</u>, establishes guidelines for probation and parole agencies. The ACA (1981: 37) standards include, for example, parole guidelines (See Table 4).

TABLE 4

SUPERVISION GUIDELINES FOR PAROLE AGENCIES

2-3166 Unless precluded by statute or court order, parole agency policy specifies that no inmate is released on parole until the parole program is verified by a designated parole officer. (Essential)

> DISCUSSION: To ensure that the inmate is being released to a legitimate parole program, policy should provide for authorizing release on parole only when the release program has been investigated and verified by a parole officer. The verification process should include field visits by the parole officer to the parolee's prospective employer, and family or friends with whom the parolee plans to reside. This investigative procedure should include the option to reject or modify the release program if circumstances warrant.

2-3167 Unless precluded by statute or court order, written policy and procedure provide that the parole agency receives pertinent information about a prospective parolee in advance of the parole date to allow for parole program development and/or verification. (Essential)

> DISCUSSION: Adequate time is needed to develop a sound program for the individual about to be paroled. In cases where the parole officer must develop a parole program, particularly where a number of community resources and relatives may be involved, early receipt of referral material is essential. Even in cases where only verification of a job and residence is needed, early receipt and completion of this task by the parole staff eases the anxiety of the inmate. The options of placing the parolee in transitional release programs, such as work

TABLE 4 (continued)

release and halfway houses, and the possible
need to advance or modify the release date to
accommodate a particular release program,
require that the parole officer receive the
referral material three months in advance of
the parole date.

2-3168 The parole agency supports release policies that
require employable inmates to have a visible means of
support or a reasonable assurance of employment, rather
than a promise of a specific job, before release on
parole. (Essential)

DISCUSSION: Often inmates cannot be released
on parole until there is a specific and
verified job waiting for them. This results in
many inmates being "overdue," or retained past
their parole date in the institution. This is
an expensive policy, both in terms of
institutional costs and inmate anxiety and
motivation. Family help, public assistance,
halfway house placement, and direct financial
assistance can maintain parolees adequately
until they are self-supporting. A number of
studies have shown that releasing parolees with
"reseasonable assurance" of employment does not
adversely affect recidivism rates, and that
offenders do as well or better if they can find
their own jobs.

Confidentiality

Problems arise for the probation or parole officer
who does not follow ethical and agency standards. The
responsible probation officer, for example, does not
usually encourage any "off the record" statements by a
defendant upon whom he or she is conducting a presentence
investigation. If the probation officer listens to an
"off the record" statement in which a defendant describes
another crime he or she committed, but was not arrested,
the officer is faced with a dilemma of reporting or
failing to report an additional past crime. This places
the officer in the position of a law enforcement officer
which includes duties beyond his/her primary area of
responsibility.

Another problem area would concern the discussion of a presentence investigation outside the office. Professional probation officers do not talk about investigations in public or to non-privileged parties. This could constitute a serious ethical violation and possibly result in actions and directives by the court.

The probation officer might face a different ethical question if he or she is assigned to conduct a presentence investigation on a relative. The ethical probation officer will ask that the presentence investigation be assigned to a different probation officer, since his/her objectivity might be questioned. A probation or parole officer, much like a judge, should avoid, if possible, even the appearance of impropriety.

TEXT OVERVIEW

Probation and Parole in Practice is designed to provide the reader with an overview and description of probation and parole systems, and to assist in the development of skills for applying basic knowledge and concepts in practice. The organization of this text reflects this purpose. First, a brief examination is made of the early introduction of probation and parole to America. Second, an overview of both the organization and operation of the federal and state systems is detailed. The analysis of the organizational structure serves to describe the role and resources of probation and parole systems as an important component of the broader criminal justice system. Similarly an examination of the operation of probation and parole systems assists in promoting an understanding of their essential dynamics. Third, the numerous duties and responsibilities of probation and parole officers are focused upon, indicating the variety of endeavors expected and required of these individuals. Fourth, attention is directed to the effective application of counseling and treatment techniques in the probation and parole setting. These techniques are of increasing importance to professionals in the performance of their jobs which stress effective counseling skills. Fifth, an examination of future trends and issues in probation and parole is made to promote an awareness of future developments and demonstrate how they will impact the future delivery of services. Finally, a special question and exercise section is included to evaluate the reader's ability to actually perform some of the major responsibilities of probation and parole officers. With this improved understanding and familiarity of the probation and parole systems, it is anticipated that the reader will be better able to realistically appraise, and function within, America's probation and parole systems.

References

American Correctional Association. (1966). Manual of correctional standards. Washington, DC: Author.

American Correctional Association. (1981). Standards for adult probation and parole field services. (2nd ed.). Rockville, MD: Author.

American justice: ABC's of how it really works. (1982, November 1). U.S. News & World Report.

American Law Institute. (1962). Model penal code. Philadelphia: Author.

Carney, L. P. (1977). Corrections and the community. Englewood Cliffs, NJ: Prentice-Hall.

Dillingham, S. D. & Montgomery, R. H., Jr. (1982, October). Can riots be prevented? Corrections Today, 44 (5), 50-52, 54-56.

Dressler, D. (1969). Practice and theory of probation and parole (2nd ed.). New York: Columbia University Press.

Fox, V. (1972, August). Prison riots in a democratic society. Police, 16, 35.

Gallup, G. (1982, May). Prisons: Americans favor rehabilitation over punishment. The Gallup Report, No. 200.

Montgomery, R. H., Jr.(1974). A measurement of inmate satisfaction/dissatisfaction in selected South Carolina correctional institutions. Unpublished doctoral dissertation, University of South Carolina, Columbia.

Moos, Rudolph H. (1975). Evaluating correctional and community settings. New York: John Wiley & Sons.

National Advisory Commission on Criminal Justice Standards and Goals. (1973). Report on corrections. Washington, DC: U.S. Government Printing Office.

National Council on Crime and Delinquency. (1972). Policies and background information. Hackensack, NJ: Author.

South Carolina Department of Parole and Community Corrections. (1981). South Carolina parole and community corrections board annual report. Columbia, SC: Author.

U. S. Department of Justice. (1939). Attorney General's survey of release procedures. Washington, DC: U.S. Government Printing Office.

U.S. Department of Justice. (1982). Probationers in the United States. Washington, DC: U.S. Government Printing Office.

Wenk, E. A. & Moos, R. H. (1972, July). Social climates in prison: An attempt to conceptualize and measure environmental factors in total institutions. Journal of Research in Crime and Delinquency, 9, 141.

Chapter 2

THE EVOLUTION OF PROBATION AND PAROLE

LEARNING OBJECTIVES

* Trace the history of probation practices.

* Trace the history of parole practices.

* Explain the American contributions to probation and parole.

* Outline recent developments and issues in modern probation and parole practices.

DISCUSSION QUESTIONS

1. What role did early English history play in the developments of probation and parole?

2. How did probation and parole practices differ in their development?

3. To what extent have modern probation and parole practices been accepted as alternatives to imprisonment in the United States?

4. What recent improvements have been experienced in probation and parole systems?

IMPORTANT TERMS

Benefit of clergy	"Earned work" credit
Recognizance	"Good time" credit
Surety	"Ticket-of-leave"
Common law	Parole boards
Equity law	Resource brokerage
Filing of cases	Prediction model

NAMES TO REMEMBER

Athelstane	Col. Montesinos
Matthew Hill	Alexander Maconochie
John Augustus	George Obermaier
Peter Thacker	William Crofton

THE ORIGIN AND HISTORY OF PROBATION

In tracing the evolution, acceptance and implementation of probation theories and practices, attention is generally focused upon at least four major developments which served to transform traditional orientations toward punishment into more rehabilitative goals. This progression was slow and began with the expanded use of numerous common law antecedents to probation, such as benefit of clergy, judicial reprieve, release on personal recognizance and others. A second important stage in the development of modern concepts of probation was the introduction of innovative probation practices to America by John Augustus in 1841. This introduction initiated a movement in America which led to a recognition of the probation officer as a bonafide professional occupation. Finally, the employment and utilization of probation officers grew nationally, resulting in the state and federal probation systems as Americans know them today.

Early English Developments

England, like most early European civilizations, experienced a harsh and violent history throughout the Middle Ages. Nowhere was this condition more evident than in the treatment of criminals, who were typically subjected to trial by combat or ordeal. Nevertheless, over a period of centuries, a variety of practices gradually evolved which served to ameliorate the severity of punishment practices.

One of the earliest recorded forms of relief granted to English subjects was a declaration of Athelstane, the Anglo-Saxon King (895-940), that forbade the execution of anyone under the age of 15 years. King Athelstane also instituted an early type of "bail" system in which an offender could be released to a responsible person providing surety and monitoring the offender's behavior (Smith & Berlin, 1979).

A second common law antecedent of probation which evolved in England was a privilege known as benefit of clergy. This device emerged during the reign of Henry II, in the 1200's. The practice originally permitted arrested clergy (later including all persons capable of reading, and some who could "fake" the skill), to have their cases transferred to ecclesiastical courts for disposition. By claiming benefit of clergy, which included the recitation of a biblical passage, a lenient sentence would typically be received, as opposed to the traditional death sentence of a secular court. Many illiterates qualified for this privilege by memorizing a passage from the psalm Miserere me ("Have mercy on me"). This practice was introduced to America where it was accepted prior to the American Revolutionary War (Henningsen, 1981). The benefit of clergy was officially abolished for commoners in England in 1827, and dealt its final death blow in 1841, when it was terminated for aristocrats as well.

The practice of recognizance, or "binding over for good behavior," was a practice which gained acceptance in the fourteenth century English courts. Similar to Athelstane's original concept, this process allowed an offender to escape conviction through release to another person who stood as surety or supplied bail. Such release was contingent upon continued good behavior, and required supervision and monitoring by the person acting as surety. The first recorded use of recognizance in the United States occurred in 1830 in the case of Commonwealth v. Chase, heard in the Municipal Court of Boston (Callison, 1983). In this case, Judge Peter Oxenbridge Thacker heard a guilty plea by the defendant, Jerusha Chase. The judge released the defendant at the request of her friends, but the offender was subject to return to the court at its insistence. The rationale for this sentence was to guarantee future compliance with the law (Hussey & Duffee, 1980). In 1836, Massachusetts passed a statute which permitted the release of petty offenders on their own recognizance. Increased reliance upon bail also became an accepted practice during this period. In instances where release on one's own recognizance appeared inappropriate, bail provided additional guarantees for court appearance by mandating sureties. These sureties became responsible for the defendant's supervision. As a result, release on one's own recognizance and bail evolved into valuable techniques for early probation efforts.

Judicial reprieve, another forerunner of probation, experienced a gradual and circuitous acceptance as an official judicial procedure in England. As the English courts developed a sophisticated "Common Law" (based upon judge-made law through use of precedents), a parallel system of "Equity Law" emerged. Equity was administered by a royal chancellor who was authorized to issue decrees based upon then developing principles of equity, such as injunctive relief. By the sixteenth century, a common law system of both law and equity, with overlapping principles, was firmly in place. Judicial reprieve, involving the suspension of a sentence, was one device

TABLE 5

THE EVOLUTION OF PROBATION: KEY DEVELOPMENTS

895-940   Anglo-Saxon King (Athelstane) pioneered bail
           by surety

1200's   "Benefit of clergy" evolved during reign of
           Henry II

1300's   English courts practiced recognizance
           ("binding over for good behavior")

1827   "Benefit of clergy" officially abolished in
           England

1830   Practice of "binding over" introduced in
           United States

1836   Massachusetts passed statute allowing for use
           of recognizance

1841   English barrister, Matthew Hill, instituted
           suspended sentences

1841   John Augustus ("The Father of Probation" in
           United States) began probation work

1878   Professional probation oficers hired in
           Boston, Massachusetts

1880   Statewide authorization of probation officers
           in Massachusetts

1987-9   Missouri, Vermont, Rhode Island, Illinois and
           Minnesota pass original probation
           legislation

1907   National Association of Probation Officers
           (NPA) formed in Minneapolis, Minnesota.

1911   NAPO expanded into National Probation
           Association (NPA)

1916   U. S. Supreme Court overruled federal court
           authority to suspend sentences

1925   President Coolidge established Federal
           Probation System

1940   Federal probation transferred from Federal
           Bureau of Prisons to Administrative Office of
           the United States Courts

that developed from this body of law. A judge who had reservations about the verdict of a trial could grant a reprieve enabling the offender to seek a conditional or absolute pardon at a later date. Some courts would grant a reprieve and impose conditions of transportation to a colony. This device came to viewed as a precedent for the modern practice of suspending sentences.

Judicial practices known as "filing of cases" gained acceptance in Massachusetts during the nineteenth century. This practice usually occurred in cases involving mitigating circumstances or cases where an appellate decision relating to the case was anticipated. It involved suspending the imposition of sentence after a verdict of guilty (Henningsen, 1981). Both the defendant and the prosecutor were required to consent to the filing. By delaying the imposition of a final judgement, a defendant's case might never reach a final verdict (Smith & Berlin, 1979). This device provided the leverage for making a defendant's freedom dependent upon continued good behavior.

Probation Introduced to America

When examining the introduction of probation practices in America, brief mention must be made of a simultaneous development in England. In 1841, an English barrister and magistrate of the City of Birmingham, England--Matthew Davenport Hill--instituted a practice of completely suspending sentences for youthful offenders by placing them under the supervision of approved adults or guardians. This "rehabilitative" approach depended upon the assistance of local police in monitoring the behavior of the "probationed" juveniles, although it lacked a formal mechanism for revoking the privilege or reinstituting the original sentence. Still, it has come to be recognized as a precursor to the modern concept of probation.

The year 1841, however, is better known for developments in America which formally introduced probation in the criminal justice systems of the world. It was in that year that John Augustus, considered to be the true "father of probation," began probation practices which serve as the foundation for contemporary probation systems.

John Augustus, born in Massachusetts (1784), became a successful businessman at an early age. In addition, he had a strong sense of public service and civic responsibility which he later directed toward the rehabilitation of criminal offenders. In 1841, at the age of 57, Augustus began his "probation" career. As he was leaving a courthouse upon delivering a pair of boots to a judge, a "ragged and wretched looking" man was brought in for sentencing. The man had been found guilty of being a "common drunkard." Augustus spoke with the man before sentence was passed and felt that the man desired to be reformed. To be saved from the House of Correction, the man agreed to refrain from future drinking. To the shock of the court, John Augustus offered bail for the man and suggested a period of probation. The judge accepted the proposal and ordered the man to return in three weeks. After three weeks, Augustus accompanied the man back to court. The former "drunkard" was clean-shaven, well-dressed, and had refrained from alcohol consumption. The judge, impressed by Augustus' results, fined the man only one cent plus court fees for his crime (Augustus, 1852).

Because of Augustus's efforts and hard work, it soon became a rule of the court in Boston that a person charged with being a common drunkard, could be granted probation. Augustus eventually enlarged the scope of his work to include juvenile and female offenders.

John Augustus' duties increased as he became responsible for: finding temporary homes for the destitute; feeding and clothing the needy; and helping to find work for those who could be employed. He provided additional assistance to thousands of neglected and homeless women. His work was done on a purely voluntary basis, eventually leading to the failure of his own business. He spent much of his money on bails and fines for his "charges." Recognizing the worth of his endeavors, his friends assisted him financially, thus enabling him to continue his philanthropic work. The records of John Augustus' service reveal the effectiveness of his work. Of his first 1,100 recorded cases, only one failure was recorded. Of the more than 2,000 people he bailed, only 10 proved ungrateful or absconded. Much of his success was attributed to his personal involvement and fundamentally sound probationary techniques.

There were five fundamental steps in Augustus' approach to probation, which laid the foundation of many modern probation systems. First, the sentence was suspended. Second, the defendant was granted conditional liberty. Third, some sort of supervision with conditions was devised. Fourth, revocation of probation was implemented for breach of any conditions. Finally, there was a careful screening of candidates for service. In the performance of these steps, Augustus soon discovered various factors needed to be considered. Screening became extremely important. In the selection of a probationer, Augustus would consider the previous character of the person, his or her age, how promising the person's future looked, and whether or not it was a first offense. Once a person was placed on probation, Augustus performed many additional duties. He was required to note the general conduct of the probationer, as well as to make sure the person attended school or engaged in honest employment. He often arranged living accommodations, and even maintained a careful register of all the cases he handled. Augustus made impartial, honest reports to the court concerning the probationer when requested. The practices of John Augustus—which included investigating cases, interviewing clients, supervising releases, and providing services for the probationer—were later accepted as basic techniques in almost all probation systems.

The innovativeness and farsightedness of Augustus were not always recognized, and reform did not always come without a price. As well as suffering the hardships of monetary failings, Augustus was faced with a great deal of personal opposition. Law enforcement resented losing the normal monetary "lock-up fee." The fact that he was providing bail "in all proper cases" also annoyed many of the clerks, officers, and prosecutors, who attempted to sway public opinion against him and his reform. Some people even believed that his methods were only incentives to crime and called him a mock philanthropist. Still, Augustus remained steadfast through it all, gathering support from judges and the press, and eventually, many of the citizenry.

Probation Develops as a Profession

Early probation practices, modeled after those pioneered by John Augustus, gained a gradual but steady acceptance after Augustus' death. In 1878, the city of Boston hired its first probation officer who worked under the supervision of the municipal police with both male and female offenders. Following a two year trial period, the Massachusetts legislature, in 1880, approved the nation's first statewide hiring of probation officers. The law removed probation officers from the employment of police departments (Henningsen, 1981).

Following the example of Massachusetts, Missouri became the second state to enact a probation law, in 1897. In Missouri's legislation, the prerequisites for receiving a sentence of probation were numerous and the term "parole" was used synonymously for probation. This legislation may be viewed as the forerunner of modern probation statutes, frequently fraught with confusion and complexity. In 1898, Vermont enacted probation laws which were county-based. Rhode Island, on the other hand, adopted a state administered system in 1899. Illinois and Minnesota also passed probation statutes in 1899, although they were limited to juveniles (Smith and Berlin, 1979). As a result, by 1900 numerous states had recognized probation as a profession and had implemented to varying degrees, probation offices to fulfill the newly recognized occupation.

The national use of probation was enhanced by developments in the juvenile court movement, beginning in 1899 with the states of Illinois, Minnesota and Colorado enacting new laws for use in juvenile cases. By 1925 every state had some type of probation alternative for juveniles, although it was not until 1967 that all the states in the United States had laws authorizing probation for adults (Smith & Abadinsky, 1982).

In 1907 a small group of probation officers met in Minneapolis to form a National Association of Probation Officers. By 1911 the group had reorganized under the name of the National Probation Association (NPA). The NPA has since evolved into the current National Council on Crime and Delinquency (NCCD), which publishes the Crime and Delinquency journal.

While most states had authorized probation alternatives during the early 1900's, the United States government had not passed such laws for the federal courts, and the authority of the federal courts to grant probationary sentences came into question. In 1916 the U. S. Supreme Court decided the question in the landmark Killets decision (Ex parte United States, 24 U.S 27, 37 S.Ct. 72, 61 L. Ed. 129). In this decision, the U. S. Supreme Court decided that the federal courts had no power to indefinitely suspend a defendant's sentence. To indefinitely suspend sentences, the court reasoned, would be a refusal to enforce the law. Such a refusal would constitute usurping legislative powers. By refusing to recognize such a judicial power, the court explicitly recognized the power of the legislative branch to enact such laws. By 1925, probation advocates were able to convince Congress of the need for such legislation.

The Federal Probation Act was passed by Congress in 1925 and signed by President Coolidge. It officially established the Federal Probation System. In 1930 two changes were made to this legislation which had a substantial impact on the system's development. One change removed the system from the U. S. Civil Service and placed it under the power of the federal district courts with the power of appointment of probation officers, while the second change extended supervisory responsibilities for parolees to probation officers (Federal Judicial Center, 1976).

In 1940 the Federal Probation System underwent another important change by transferring its authority from the Bureau of Prisons in the U. S. Department of Justice to the Administrative Office of the United States Courts. This shift from the executive branch to the judicial branch was hotly debated for numerous years, but further attempts to transfer the office failed. While an argument existed for combining all agencies dealing with corrections under one department, a countervailing interest of insulating probation from the influences of the prosecution side was recognized.

THE ORIGIN AND HISTORY OF PAROLE

The origin and history of parole like that of probation had its roots in early English practices and experienced a gradual development until the nineteenth century. During the 1800's significant contributions were made by several countries. In 1870 the concept of parole began to receive acceptance in the United States. The term "parole" is derived from a French expression which means "conditional liberation" and was developed as a procedure which permitted the early release of an inmate from prison on a conditional basis. If the inmate failed to fulfill the parole requirements, his or her sentence could be reimposed. Evolving over a 75 year period, this device eventually gained acceptance in the United States as a necessary supplement to, and alternative for, incarceration.

Early English Practices

As early as 1597, England had passed laws which punished dangerous criminals by banishing them from their homeland. Such an approach to the problem of crime was common for the age and by the seventeenth century the practice of transporting criminals from England had

TABLE 6

THE EVOLUTION OF PAROLE: KEY DEVELOPMENTS

1597   English law provided for banishment of dangerous criminals

1655   English law nullified pardons for returning prisoners

1670   Virginia court banned importation of criminals to colony

1787   Australia established as a colony for transported criminals

1790   England authorized colonies to remit or shorten criminal sentences

1811   England authorized work credit to reduce prescribed sentence length

1817   New York passed first "good time" law, shortening terms of imprisonment

1821   England adopted guidelines for awarding "work credit"

1835   Col. Montesinos instituted sentence reduction for good behavior in Valencia, Spain

1840   Englishman Alexander Maconochie ("Father of Parole") instituted parole concepts in Australia

1842   German prison head, Obermaier, initiated prison reforms reducing recidivism in Munich

1853   English Penal Servitude Act of 1853 formalized conditional releases

1854   Sir William Crofton, head of Irish prisons, enacted prisoner classification system

1867   Transportation of prisoners to Australia terminated

1870   American Prison Association introduced Crofton reforms to United States

1876   Elmira Reformatory (NY) adopted concept of parole supervison

TABLE 6 (continued)

1884   Ohio extended parole throughout state prison
        system

1913   Wisconsin passed Huber law, permitting inmates to
        support dependents

1944   Last state adopted parole system--Mississippi

_____

become commonplace. Not only were dangerous criminals
transported, but due to harsh economic conditions and
high unemployment, many others suffered the ordeal. The
English parliament expressly authorized the shipment of
many criminals to the American colonies in hopes of
supplying direly needed manpower (Smith & Berlin,
1979). To create an incentive for the transported
convicts to provide such labor, the prisoners were
granted pardons and clemency for their crimes. A problem
soon arose, however, when some of the pardoned criminals
managed to surreptitiously return to England. As a
result, in 1655 a law was passed nullifying all pardons
for prisoners returning to England and subjecting them to
execution. The transported criminals in America did not
always passively accept their fate and in 1670,
encouraged a rebellion among slaves in Virginia. In
response to this uprising, a Virginia court issued a
directive prohibiting any further importation of
criminals. The effort was futile, of course, and the
practice continued until the American Revolutionary War.

Although the Revolutionary War ended the importation
of English criminals to the United States, it marked the
beginning of transporting offenders to Australia. In
1787, Prime Minister Pitt established Australia as a
colony for criminals only 17 years after the continent's
discovery by Captain Cook. Unlike the preceding
banishment practices with America, the English government
did not relinquish control of the prisoners sent to
Australia. The government paid all transportation
expenses and assigned the prisoners to the local governor
with "property in service" rights, a form of involuntary
servitude. These rights were normally reassigned by
contract to free settlers. In 1790, however, a special
provision was passed which empowered the Australian
governors to remit or shorten the sentences of the
imported convicts. While some convicts received absolute

pardons at first, a process of granting "tickets-of-leave," or conditional pardons, soon became the standard practice. The ticket-of-leave was very similar to a grant of freedom for an indentured servant. It enabled the individual to legally accept employment and entitled the person to various privileges, such as the freedom to marry.

The ticket-of-leave practice was modified in 1811 in a manner which permitted transported criminals to work-off a prescribed sentence (a forerunner of modern "earned work" and "good-time" credits). This concept found root in America, as evidenced by the passage of a "good-time" law in New York in 1817, which authorized a shortened term of imprisonment to reward good conduct. In 1821 specific minimum sentences were assigned in England which enabled convicts to serve a finite number of years, knowing that freedom would follow although only a portion of the original sentence was served. Some of these minimum sentences reduced the original sentence by as much as one-half.

Acceptance and Expansion of Parole

The role of early English practices in shaping parole comprises an important correctional influence, but not an exclusive one. Not to be overlooked were the contributions of other European countries, notably Spain, Germany and Ireland.

In 1835, the governor (warden) of the prison at Valencia, Spain -- Col. Montesinos -- instituted a plan emphasizing discipline, vocational training and education which provided for a one-third reduction in sentence length for good behavior and personal progress. Following implementation of these reforms, recidivism at the Valencia prison decreased from 35 percent to almost none, indicating a highly successful and well-managed program of treatment (Killinger & Cromwell, 1977).

During the period when Col. Montesinos was experiencing success in Spain, an Englishman--Alexander Maconochie--was applying his own ideas to the penal system, earning him the title of "the father of parole." In 1837 Maconochie made a proposal to the English parliament to modify penal policy by requiring the length of a convicts criminal sentence to hinge upon the individuals demonstrated "good behavior and industry." Records were to be kept to measure each convict's progress. The system had numerous additional innovations including: (1) public inmate trials with procedural safeguards; (2) improved living environments and social amenities; (3) a "mark system" whereby inmates earned money as work incentives; and (4) a five-stage program of "graduated release," culminating in full freedom for successful inmates. In 1840 Maconochie assumed the role of Governor of an Australian penal colony where his experimental reforms were tested over a four year period of tenure. Gradually, criticism of his methods increased until he was forced to resign his position, preventing any final determination regarding the long-term success of his reforms.

George Obermaier, a German contemporary of Montesinos and Maconochie, served as governor of a Munich prison in 1842. Upon assuming supervision of a crowded and rebellious prison population, he instituted numerous successful rehabilitative reforms centered upon earning the confidence and respect of the inmates. Much of the credit for his success was largely attributed to the indefinite sentences his inmates faced and the close supervision practices imposed on discharged inmates.

The Penal Servitude Act of 1853 was passed in England giving legal status to the ticket-of-leave system, for the purpose of creating an alternative plan to the compulsory transportation of inmates to Australia. In many cases the plan called for a minimum period of incarceration prior to receiving a ticket-of-leave. The objectives of enticing inmates to engage in good behavior and making their release conditional, were not usually met by this poorly administered (though well conceived) plan.

In 1854, Sir William Crofton became Director of the Irish Prison System and began a new method of administering the ticket-of-leave device. Under his direction, tickets-of-leave were awarded only to inmates demonstrating desirable attitudes and proven accomplishments. Among the features of Crofton's system were the following: (1) Maconochie's supervised stages of imprisonment; (2) indeterminate sentences; (3) improved prison conditions; (4) supervised release; and (5) public confidence. Perhaps due to the emphasis on public support, Crofton's accomplishments received widespread recognition and acceptance.

The English practice of transporting prisoners to Australia underwent modification as the settlers increased their protests, similar to events in the American colonies. The English government responded by initiating a "selection system" of training prisoners before being transported. An assigned "board" (precursor to modern "parole boards") was used to evaluate inmate readiness. Ultimately, the progran failed and, in 1867, England ended transportation of convicts to Australia.

Parole Development in the United States

The American parole system naturally drew most of its impetus and ideas from the European experiences. Still, many of the key developments had distinctive American qualities and even came to later serve as models for European reforms. One landmark event occurring in America in 1870 was the National Congress of the recently organized American Prison Association, which advocated a philosophy of rehabilitation based upon the principles Crofton had implemented in the Irish prisons. The participants issued a "Declaration of Principles" on prison reform which incorporated many widely held ideas in contemporary society, including: (1) rehabilitation as a goal of incarceration; (2) a progressive classification of prisons; (3) a system rewarding good behavior in prison; (4) an evaluation of prisoner reformation; and (5) comprehensive programs of supervision and assistance upon release from prison.

One response to the 1870 conference was the establishment of Elmira Reformatory in 1876 which included a system of parole supervision. Prisoners were carefully selected for parole; indeterminate sentences enhanced rehabilitation; privileges were dependent upon behavior and progress; organization and discipline were enforced; and requirements for parole had to be met. Once paroled, the parolees had to report monthly to their assigned guardian who supervised their activities. Prison reformer Zebulon Brockway served as the Elmira superintendent and is credited with having insured much of the program's success.

Following the example at Elmira, parole systems were soon adopted by the other states, although sentencing reforms lagged behind. In 1884, Ohio became the first state to extend parole throughout its state prison system (Parker, 1975). By 1922, the number of states with parole statutes increased to 45. Meanwhile, the state of Wisconsin passed the Huber Law in 1913, a much needed statute which allowed jailed inmates to support their dependents for the first time. Finally, in 1944, Mississippi became the last state to adopt parole. Sentencing schemes, however, still varied among the states.

MODERN PROBATION AND PAROLE PRACTICES

As the history of probation and parole reveals, today's practices evolved over a number of centuries and have precedents in numerous countries. Yet, modern probation and parole practices in the United States have a number of distinctly American features. The following discussion will present a brief analysis of some of the recent developments experienced in probation and parole systems, some of the pressing issues confronting the systems, and several innovative features of the systems which deserve closer attention.

Recent Developments in Probation and Parole

How have the changes since the impact of John Augustus shaped probation and parole today? The best method for assessing the current dimensions of probation and parole today is to view the growth that has accompanied each practice and to identify major developments and trends.

In 1966 the Task Force on Corrections noted that: "probation in the United States is administered by hundreds of independent agencies operating under a different law in each state and under widely varying philosophies, often within the same state" (Task Force on Corrections, 1966: 28). In 1978 the U. S. Bureau of Census found that over 1900 agencies offered adult probation services and more than 2100 agencies provided juvenile probation services. In both cases, over 55% of the services were offered on the state level with the rest being offered at the county or municipal level (Abadinsky, 1982).

The use of probation has also experienced increasing acceptance as an alternative to incarceration. In 1980, of all adults processed through the criminal justice system, approximately 60% were given probation as opposed to the remaining 40% who were incarcerated (Bartollas, 1981). The probation profession has also grown significantly with over 36,000 practicing probation officers by 1976 (Callison, 1983). Today, 11 states operate on a county basis, the remaining 39 are statewide. Thirteen of the statewide systems retain a combined state/county service delivery system.

The administration of parole is comparatively simple in organization, since it generally consists of one agency per state. Still, there are two basic models for administering parole services. Under one model parole

authority is granted to an independent parole board,
while a second approach gives parole authority to the
respective corrections agency. Both approaches have
advantages and disadvantages and the optimum approach may
well depend upon the current operations and leadership
within the corrections or parole authority (Task Force on
Corrections, 1966). In all settings parole is a function
of the executive branch of government (Henningsen, 1981).

Current Issues in Probation and Parole

What are the problems and issues in the field of
probation and parole work? A National Institute of
Justice publication brings into focus issues in probation
and parole which include: (1) consideration of the
termination of parole as a release alternative; (2) the
possible release of all offenders under some form of
supervision similar to parole; (3) probation agencies
having to provide a growing range of services to an
increasing number of clients, frequently without an
increase in resources; (4) demands for probation to
provide both pretrial services and for misdemeanant
probation; and (5) demands that probation agencies
assume a surveillance rather than a treatment posture
(University Research Corp., 1980: 13).

A nationwide survey of probation administrators
identified the following issues as being of paramount
concern to the profession: (1) increasingly scarce
resources; (2) higher numbers of offenders; (3) more
severe offenders on probation; (4) longer sentences; (5)
judicial pressure for accountability; (6) poor image of
probation services; (7) lack of knowledge about program
effectiveness; (8) lack of agreement of outcome
measures; and (9) inadequate use of management skills
(University Research Corp., 1980).

In summary, the modern probation and parole officer
must essentially act as a "resource broker." The officer
must assess the needs of the client; find the community
resources to deal with the particular problem(s) of the
client; and make a contract with the community agency to
provide the service for the client.

Prediction Models

The modern probation and parole officer must be
familiar with prediction models. These models provide a
method to utilize past experiences systematically. These
models help a probation officer in writing a presentence
recommendation; in deciding what level of supervision a

probationer or parolee should be under; and on predicting
when an inmate will be eligible for parole consideration.

Using such a model, for example, the probation
officer is able to statistically predict how a defendant
is likely to behave if placed on probation. If the
prediction model predicts the defendant will succeed on
probation, the probation officer may recommend that the
judge sentence the defendant to a period of probation.

Research conducted nationwide by the Comptroller
General revealed that models were more successful in
predicting behavior than the subjective feelings of
probation officers. The models may vary in form. The
following table demonstrates a typical prediction model,
accompanied by a success rate scale.

TABLE 7

ILLUSTRATIVE PREDICTIVE MODEL

Significant Characteristics	Model Value	Individual's Score
No history of opiate use	9	--
Family has no criminal history	6	--
Not an alcoholic	6	--
Married	4	--
No prior arrests	4	--
Total possible score for probationer	29	--

SUMMARY RISK TABLE

Score	Success Rate	Individual's Assessment
23-29	(90%)	--
10-22	(70%)	--
00-09	(10%)	--

Source: State and County Probation: Systems in Crisis, 1976.

34

Salient factor scores are used in the prediction models of the U. S. Parole Commission to measure the amount of time a federal prisoner will serve in prison before being considered for parole. The higher the salient factor score the less time a federal prisoner must serve, as compared to a federal prisoner with the same charge but a lower salient factor score. A federal prisoner's salient factor score is based on his prior criminal record, employment history; drug history and family situation.

Change: A Continuing Process

The modern probation and parole officer is aware that model guidelines can be changed depending upon the philosophy of the public or public officials. A news article in 1983 illustrated how easily guidelines can be changed. In an interview with the U.S. Parole Commissioner concerning recent changes, the following comments were made: " The Reagan Administration, having failed to get Congress to eliminate paroles for federal prisoners, issued tough, new parole guidelines . . . designed to keep violent criminals and offenders in prison longer." (The (S.C.) State, Jan. 25).

The highlights of the article included a number of new penalties and envisioned impacts: (a) the minimum time to be served by those convicted of specified violent crimes will nearly double; (b) the amount of time to be served by drug dealers will significantly increase; (c) mandatory sentences will be eventually phased in to replace parole eligibility in general; (d) overcrowded federal prisons will increase in population; (e) guidelines for classifying the seriousness levels of criminal behavior will be modified to reflect the current disdain for particular violent activities; and (f) minimum sentences for most offenders will be increased. The Commissioner pointed out that parole decisions will continue to be made on two primary factors: the severity of the offense and the risk that a convict might return to crime. That risk is measured largely on the basis of the inmate's prior criminal record.

If agents of change are underestimated, dysfunctional consequences may occur within an organization (More, 1977). Since probation and parole is currently experiencing enormous pressures critical to its future development, recognition of programmatic needs and new coping strategies are of increasing importance.

Volunteers: A New Resource

Although probation work originated from the volunteer work of John Augustus in the 1840's, the modern probation and parole officer is still aware of the value of the volunteer. Until the 1960's, little attention was directed toward the use of volunteers or paraprofessionals in probation and parole operations (Smith & Berlin, 1976).

Scheier (1970) points out the many services a volunteer can perform including: (a) acting as behavior models for probationers; (b) assisting probationers in finding employment; (c) helping to recruit and train other volunteers; (d) acting as tutors for probationers with limited reading ability; and (e) offering many other talents and forms of assistance. A major task of the modern probation officer is the recruiting, selecting, and training of volunteers. The college student, for example, who takes advantage of the opportunity to work as a volunteer, greatly increases his/her understanding of the criminal justice system and develops special professional skills applicable to numerous employment opportunities.

SUMMARY

Probation and parole, related but dissimilar concepts, experienced a roughly parallel yet circuitous historical development and professional acceptance in America. Both probation and parole practices evolved from a number of early English, common law antecedents. Similarly, both concepts were embraced in America during the 1800's, reflecting recognition of their successful, though limited usage abroad. As the nation and American criminal justice system expanded, a need for professionalized treatment and management of a growing offender population was recognized. Progressive thinking individuals, groups, and federal/state/local governments soon realized the importance of developing formalized, professional systems for implementing probation and parole practices.

Today, probation and parole comprise essential elements of our overall criminal justice system. Both include comprehensive guidelines and regulations, and are administered by professional staffs. Although the administrative authorities for each may differ among the states, most appear to be experiencing shared pressures and concerns in areas of development, change and management of resources. In meeting the challenges

modern probation and parole practices have incorporated
new features and techniques, ranging from prediction
models to increased reliance upon volunteerism. In all
liklihood, further innovations will occur as new problems
and pressures surface.

References

Abadinsky, H. (1982). Probation and parole: Theory and
practice (2nd ed.). Englewood Cliffs, NJ: Prentice-
Hall.

Augustus, J. (1852 reprint). A report of the labors of
John Augustus. Haddam, CT: Connecticut Criminal
Justice Training Academy.

Bartollas, C. (1981). Introduction to corrections. New
York: Harper and Row Publishers.

Callison, H. G. (1983). Introduction to community-based
corrections. New York: McGraw-Hill, Inc.

Federal Judicial Center. (1976). An introduction to the
federal probation system. Washington, DC: Author.

Henningsen, R. J. (1981). Probation and parole. New
York: Harcourt Brace, Jovanovich.

Hussey, F. A. & Duffee, D. E. (1980). Probation, parole,
and community field services: Policy, structure and
process. New York: Harper and Row.

Killinger, G. G. & Cromwell, P. F., Jr. (1978).
Corrections in the community: Alternatives to
imprisonment (2nd ed.). St. Paul: West Publishing.

More, H. W., Jr. (1977). Criminal justice management.
St. Paul: West Publishing.

O'Leary, V. & Hanrahan, K. J. (1977). Parole systems in
the United States (3rd ed.). Hackensack, NJ:
National Council on Crime and Delinquency.

Parker, W. (1975) Parole. College Park, MD: American
Correctional Association.

Scheier, I. H. (1970, June). The volunteer in probation.
Federal Probation.

37

Smith, A. B. & Berline, L. (1976). Introduction to probation and parole. (1st and 2nd ed.). St. Paul: West Publishing.

Smykla, J. O. (1981). Community-based corrections: Principles and practices. New York: Macmillan Publishing.

Sniffen, M. J. (1983, January 25). New rules tighten federal paroles. The (Columbia, S. C.) State: Associated Press.

Task Force on Corrections. (1966). Task force report: Corrections. Washington, DC.: U.S. Government Printing Office.

University Research Corporation. (1979). Improved probation strategies: Trainer's handbook. Washington, DC: U.S. Government Printing Office.

Selected Readings

Carter, R. M. & Wilkins, L. T. (Eds.). (1976). Probation, parole and community corrections. New York: John Wiley and Sons.

Fox, V. (1977). Community-based corrections. Englewood Cliffs, NJ: Prentice-Hall.

Miller, E. E. & Montilla, R. M. (Eds.). (1977). Corrections in the community. Reston, Va.: Reston Publishing.

Glaser, D. (1964). The effectiveness of a prison and parole system. Indianapolis: Robbs-Merrill.

Dressler, D. (1951). Practice and theory of probation and parole. New York: Columbia University Press.

Chapter 3

ORGANIZATION AND OPERATION OF PROBATION AND PAROLE SYSTEMS

LEARNING OBJECTIVES

* Understand both the organization and operation of the federal probation and parole system.

* Be familiar with the general organizations and operations of state probation and parole systems.

* Learn the important probation and parole functions of supervision, investigation, revocation and pretrial services.

* Provide an overall comparison of federal and state probation and parole systems.

DISCUSSION QUESTIONS

1. How extensive is the federal probation and parole system, and how does it operate?

2. What other components of the criminal justice system should a probation and parole officer be familiar with? Why?

3. How significant are the budgets (including salaries) of probation and parole operations, especially when compared to other criminal justice functions?

4. Explain the supervisory and investigatory functions of probation and parole. Give examples.

5. What is parole revocation and how is it applied?

6. What is the purpose for pretrial services and how do they operate?

FEDERAL SYSTEM

Federal probation and parole services are basically standardized and uniform, resulting in a professional and qualitative level of service generally recognized as being superior to that of the state systems. Other variables important to this professionalization of services include improved resources, a reduced caseload, and a different clientele. Many state probation and parole systems consider the federal system as a model deserving emulation.

Overview of Organization and Operation

The Federal Probation System, prior to 1940, was administered by the Bureau of Prisons in the Department of Justice. The Administration of Probation was transferred to the Judiciary after the Administrative Office of the United States Courts was created on July 1, 1940. The Division of Probation, established within the Administrative Office, developed uniform standards of professional performance (e.g., standards for writing a presentence investigation). Unlike most government agencies, however, considerable autonomy is given to each of the 95 Federal District Courts. The District Courts, under the Probation Act, 18 USC 3654, have the sole power to appoint and dismiss federal probation officers. The chief probation officer in each district directs the work of all probation officers. The number of federal probation officers has increased from the first three appointments in 1927 to more than 1600 officers in 1983.

The following typically comprises the chain of command in a federal probation office: the probation officer reports to a supervisor; the supervisor reports to the deputy chief; and the deputy chief reports to the chief probation officer.

The Federal Probation Service works closely with many individuals in the federal criminal justice system. To have an effective system, there must be close working relationships between the Federal Bureau of Prisons, the U.S. Parole Commission, and the Federal Probation System. For example, federal probation officers perform parole duties in agreement with the U.S. Parole Commission. The accompanying diagram depicts the variety of persons and entities with which a federal probation officer works at various times (see Figure 1).

FIGURE 1

STAGES OF PROBATION SERVICE

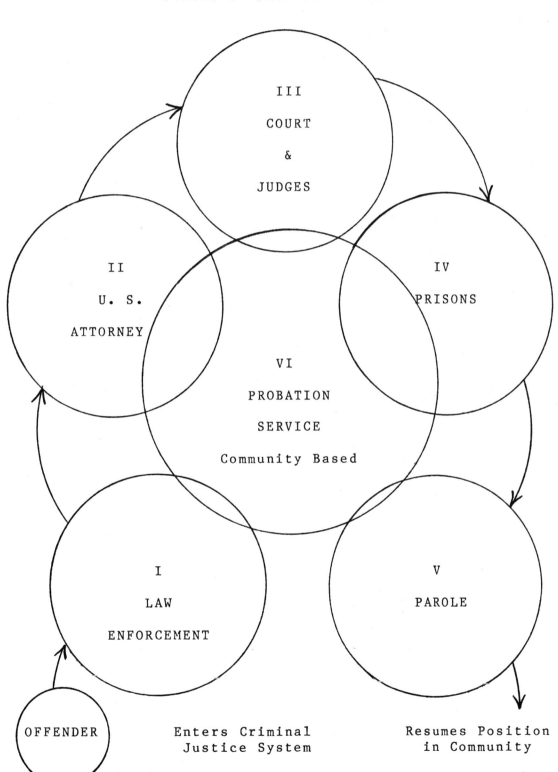

As the diagram points out, the federal probation officer (stage I) works with law enforcement officials. The probation officer, for example, may need to consult with an FBI agent who participated in the arrest of an offender who must face sentencing. The probation officer may ask the FBI agent what role the offender played in the crime.

The U.S. Attorney (stage II) is frequently contacted by a probation officer. The probation officer, for example, often requests the U.S. Attorney's help in seeking to revoke the probation of someone who has left the district without permission.

The court personnel and the federal judges (stage III) have extensive contact with probation officers. For example, the probation officer checks with court clerks to find out the exact date the defendant pleaded guilty. Federal judges, on the other hand, depend on federal probation officers to investigate the background of a defendant and recommend to the court what sentence should be imposed.

The Federal Bureau of Prisons (stage IV) contacts federal probation officers when a federal prisoner is going to be released on furlough. The federal probation officer may need to assist this person in a job search.

The Federal Probation Service (stage V) often encounters the U.S. Parole Commission. The federal probation officer at this stage may take on the role of a federal parole officer. The supervision of federal parolees is a major task. For example, annual supervision reports on all parolees must be submitted to the Federal Parole Commission.

The federal probation officer must also submit monthly statistical reports to indicate changes in his or her caseload. The probation officer who receives a new parolee to supervise indicates on his or her monthly statistical report an increase in the total number of parolees he or she is supervising. All of the statistical records on federal parolees and probationers are compiled and recorded by the Division of Probation located in Washington, D.C..

BUDGET

The financial resources to support probation and parole services are one portion of the overall expenditures of the judiciary. As Table 8 indicates, twelve cents of every budget dollar for the federal court system is spent for salaries of PO's and staff.

Federal probation officers are hired by the United States District Court in which they will work. The salary scale, however, is uniform for the entire system. Based on the recent job classification system, a new federal probation officer starts at a grade 9 and is promoted, as a general rule, to grade 11 after one year; and then to grade 12 after two years. Normally a federal probation officer will remain at grade 12 the remainder of his or her working career. The person will still be eligible for step increases in pay at the grade 12 level. If a federal probation officer is promoted to a supervisor, the person will have a grade of 13 and, if promoted to a deputy chief, a grade of 14. A chief of a federal probation district is generally a grade 15 or 16, depending on variables such as office size and approval of the Chief Judge of that district. The following are the salary ranges in federal probation as of 1983: grade 9 - $20,200; grade 11 - $24,500; grade 12 - $29,300; grade 13 - $34,900; grade 14 - $41,200; grade 15 - $48,500; grade 16 - $56,900.

TABLE 8

THE JUDICIAL DOLLAR (FISCAL YEAR 1980)

Major Expenditure Items	% of Total Expenditures
Salaries of Supporting Personnel	24
Office Space and Facilities	18
Salaries of Probation Officers and Staff	12
Salaries and Expenses, Bankruptcy Courts, Judges	10
Salaries of Judges	9
Travel Expenses	7
Fees of Jurors and Commissioners	6
Defender Services	4
Salaries and Expenses of Magistrates	4
Administrative Office and Federal Judicial Center	4
Special Courts	2
	100

Actual Total Amount: $578,761,000

Source: Administrative Office of the United States Courts, Annual Reports, 1980.

Supervision

Supervision is one of the primary responsibilities
of the federal probation officer. Table 9 describes the
types and sources of supervision over which a probation
officer is responsible.

TABLE 9

PERSONS RECEIVED FOR SUPERVISION
FOR THE TWELVE MONTH PERIODS ENDING JUNE 30, 1979 AND 1980

| | 1979 | | 1980 | |
Type of Supervision	Number	%	Number	%
Probation, District Court.	14,094	41.7	12,189	38.8
Probation, U.S. Magistrate	5,202	15.4	4,589	14.6
Pretrial Diversion........	2,255	6.7	2,015	6.4
Parole....................	6,829	20.2	7,652	24.4
Mandatory Release.........	3,222	9.5	2,671	8.5
Military Parole...........	95	0.3	226	0.7
Special Parole............	2,142	6.3	2,068	6.6
All Cases.................	33,839	100.0	31,410	100.0

Source: Administration Office of the United States
          Courts, Annual Reports, 1980, 1.

Approximately 80 % of the federal probation officers
are actively engaged in supervising probationers and
parolees. Table 10 indicates the number of officers and
their generally declining caseloads during the years 1974
- 1981.

TABLE 10

U.S. PROBATION OFFICER CASELOAD

	Officers Available for Supervision	Supervision Cases	Average Supervision Cases per Officer
1974	827	59,615	72

(TABLE 10 CONTINUED)

1975	1,129	64,261	57
1976	1,200	64,246	54
1977	1,346	64,427	48
1978	1,391	66,681	48
1979	1,390	66,087	48
1980	1,417	64,450	45
1981	1,339	59,016	44

Source: Administrative Office of the United States
Courts, Annual Reports, 1980.

Investigation

The federal probation officer is responsible for
numerous types of investigations. The annual reports of
the Administrative Office of the United States Courts
reveal that the types of investigation may vary over the
years, reflecting changes in crime, caseloads, sentencing
practices, prison populations and other variables. Table
11 indicates the types and numbers of investigations
undertaken over a three year period.

TABLE 11

INVESTIGATIVE REPORTS BY PROBATIONS OFFICER FOR THE TWELVE
MONTH PERIODS ENDING JUNE 30, 1979 & JUNE 30, 1980

Type of Investigation	1979	1980	1981
Presentence Investigation.......	26,338	23,961	24,957
Collateral Investigation for another district...........	16,506	16,836	18,501
Preliminary Investigation to assist U.S. Attorney........	3,102	2,006	2,167
Postsentence Investigation for Institution................	1,252	988	1,012
Pretransfer Investigation (Probation and Parole).........	9,944	9,561	8,928
Alleged Violation Investigation (Probation and Parole).........	11,421	12,347	12,584
Prerelease Investigation for a Federal or Military Institution....................	9,092	9,883	8,097
Special Investigation regarding a prisoner in confinement......	4,932	5,684	6,021

46

(TABLE 11 CONTINUED)

Furlough and Work-Release Reports for Bureau of Prisons Institutions............	6,239	5,925	5,920
Parole Supervision Reports......	17,284	21,824	23,066
Parole Revocation Hearing Reports..........................	1,834	1,522	1,884
Bail...............................	1,036	921	1,639
Collateral Bail..................	192	220	302
Total	109,172	111,678	115,079

Revocation

A probation or parole violation is any act or omission on the part of a probationer or parolee which is contrary to the expressed or implied conditions under which the individual is being supervised. Violations of a probationer are reported to the court and violations of a parolee reported to the U.S. Parole Commision. Otherwise, the two processes are very similar. Figure 2 illustrates such a process.

FIGURE 2

Stages of Revocation Process

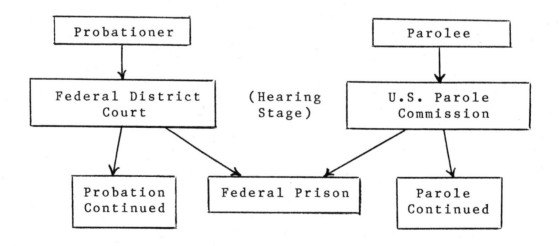

Two major court decisions have had an enormous impact on the revocation process. <u>Morrissey</u> v. <u>Brewer</u>, 408 U.S. 471 (1972) established due process rights for a parolee and required that two separate hearings be undertaken prior to revocation of parole. The Supreme Court expanded this due process requirement in 1973 in <u>Gagnon v. Scarpelli</u>, 411 U.S. 778 (1973). The court rules in this case that probationers were entitled to the same rights and procedures as parolees in revocation proceedings. In addition, the court ruled that probationers and parolees had a right to a court appointed attorney, where a need was demonstrated. A summarization of parolee rights at preliminary hearings established by the <u>Morrissey</u> decision include: (1) prior notice of the inquiry; (2) prior notice of the alleged offense; (3) right to appear in person; (4) right to present documents and witnesses; (5) right to a hearing before a neutral hearing officer; and (6) right to be given reasons for the determination made.

Those rights guaranteed at a final revocation hearing include: (1) written notice of the asserted parole violations and evidence in support thereof; (2) opportunity to be heard in person; (3) opportunity to present witnesses and documentary evidence; (4) right to confront and cross-examine adverse witnesses; (5) right to a neutral hearing body (e.g., Federal Parole Examiner); and (6) a written statement of the evidence relied on and the reasons for revoking parole.

Pretrial Services

The role of pretrial services within the overall criminal justice process is extremely important for many of the same reasons described in support of alternatives to incarceration. Although all federal probation officers are called upon to render pretrial services of various forms from time to time, Congress enacted special legislation formalizing this pretrial service on an "experimental" basis in a limited number of districts in 1974. This legislation was an important part of the Speedy Trial Act of 1974 (P.L. No. 93-619,88 Stat. 2076,18 USC 3152 <u>et seq.</u>). This act contained two titles: Title I provided a schedule for decreasing the amount of time for indictment, arraignment, and disposition of a criminal case to 100 days by July 1, 1979; Title II provided that 10 demonstration pretrial services agencies be established to interview defendants, verify information for judicial officers, and supervise and coordinate (or provide services) for certain persons on bail.

Title II of the Speedy Trial Act of 1974 authorized the Director of the Administrative Office of the United States Courts to establish, on a demonstration basis, 10 pretrial service agencies in representative judicial districts. Five of the agencies were to be governed by a seven member Board of Trustees appointed in each of the five separate districts. The agencies in the remaining selected districts were to be administered under the Probation Division of the Administrative Office of the United States Courts with the chief probation officer serving as the chief pretrial service officer.

The Act authorized the Chief Justice of the United States, with the concurrence of the Attorney General, to designate the 10 district courts in which agencies were to be established. In accordance with the criteria set forth in the statute, the Chief Justice designated that pretrial service agencies be established on a demonstration basis.

The designations were made on the basis of a study conducted by the Administrative Office of the United States Courts in accordance with the criteria established by the Speedy Trial Act. All 10 agencies were located in large metropolitan centers where the volume of criminal litigation was substantial and the types of criminal cases varied. Funds in the amount of $10 million, as authorized by the Speedy Trial Act, became available on July 1, 1975, and the task of organizing the agencies began immediately. In October 1975 the pretrial services agency in the Northern District of Illinois commenced operations, and by April 1976 pretrial agencies had been fully established in all 10 districts. Recent figures (March 10, 1982) indicate that there were 88 federal pretrial services officers in the United States. These 10 districts handled approximately 10,000 cases annually.

The pretrial service agencies generally make pre-bail investigations for judicial oficers and maintain supervision as well as provide supportive services to defendants released pending trial. More specifically, pretrial service agencies perform two basic functions: (1) the compilation and verification of background information on persons charged with the violation of federal criminal law for the use of the Federal District Judge or a United States Magistrate in setting conditions of release pursuant to the Bail Reform Act (18 U.S. Code, 3141 et seq.); and (2) the supervision of persons released from custody prior to trial or conviction, including the provision of counseling and other pretrial services. In performing these functions, the federal

pretrial services officer presents a completed form to
the Federal Judge/Magistrate which: (1) identifies the
defendant; (2) summarizes his/her history (e.g., family
ties, financial resources, health, prior record/record of
appearance); and (3) contains a recommendation. The
possible recommendations include the following options:
(a) personal recognizance, (b) unsecured bond, (c) 10%
deposit, (d) surety bond, (e) collateral, (f) third party
custody, (g) pretrial service agency supervision, and (h)
other conditions.

The stated objectives of the Speedy Trial Act were
to reduce pretrial detention and pretrial recidivism.
Included among the services to be rendered by pretrial
services agencies to persons released from custody prior
to trial or conviction were assistance in securing
necessary employment, medical, legal, or social services.
The agencies were authorized to operate, or contract for
the operation of, appropriate facilities for the custody
or care of persons released from custody. Apparent
violations of the conditions of pretrial release are
reported to the court with recommended modifications in
the terms of release. The Speedy Trial Act assumes that
pretrial service officers will cooperate with local
agencies in the performance of their duties.

The future of pretrial services has been a matter of
ongoing debate for several years. Evaluative studies
have been conducted, and proponents of different
approaches regarding the establishment of a permanent
program submitted their ideas. Generally, the studies
demonstrate many beneficial results from the program
already in operation. This past success was evidence by
the following segment of the Director's 1981 Annual
Report of the Administrative Office of th U.S. Courts:

> The Director's comprehensive report concer-
> ning the pretrial service program was submitted
> to Congress on June 19, 1979, with recommenda-
> tions that the program be made permanent in the
> demonstration districts, that it be expanded to
> other districts on the basis of demonstrated
> need, and that funds be authorized to maintain
> the program in the ten demonstration districts
> until final congressional action occurs.
> Legislation to continue and expand the pretrial
> services agencies was introduced in both Houses
> of the Congress in 1980 and passed the Senate,
> but did not pass the House. The legislation
> has been reintroduced in the 97th Congress, has
> passed the Senate again, and as of June 30,

1981, is awaiting consideration on the floor of the House. The ten demonstration programs have continued to operate through yearly authorizations and appropriations.

The Pretrial Services Act of 1982 has finally established pretrial services for each of the federal court districts (other than District of Columbia - which already had pretrial services in operation), with supervision responsibilities vested in chief probation and pretrial services officers. The functions of pretrial services includes the following:

(1) Collect, verify, and report to the judicial officer, prior to the pretrial release hearing, information pertaining to the pretrial release of each individual charged with an offense, including information relating to any danger that the release of such person may pose to any other person or the community, and recommend appropriate release conditions for such individual.

(2) Review and modify the reports and recommmendations for persons seeking release.

(3) Supervise persons released into its custody under this chapter.

(4) Operate or contract for the operation of appropriate facilities for the custody or care of persons released under this chapter including residential halfway houses, addict and alcoholic treatment centers, and counseling services.

(5) Inform the court and the United States attorney of all apparent violations of pretrial release conditions, arrests of persons released to the custody of providers of pretrial services or under the supervision of providers of pretrial services, and any danger that any such person may come to pose to any other person or the community, and recommend appropriate modifications of release conditions.

(6) Serve as coordinator for other local agencies which serve or are eligible to serve as custodians under this chapter and advise the court as to the eligibility, availability, and capacity of such agencies.

(7) Assist persons released under this chapter in securing any necessary employment, medical, legal, or social services.

(8) Prepare, in cooperation with the United States Marshall and the United States Attorney, such pretrial detention reports as are

required by the provisions of the Federal Rules of Criminal Procedure relating to the supervision of detention pending trial.

(9) Develop and implement a system to monitor and evaluate bail activities, provide information to judicial officers on the results of bail decisions, and prepare periodic reports to assist in the improvement of the bail process.

(10) To the extent provided for in an agreement between chief pretrial services officers in districts in which pretrial services are established, collect, verify, and prepare reports for the United States Attorney's office of information pertaining to the pretrial diversion of any individual who is or may be charged with an offense, and perform such other duties as may be required under any such agreement.

(11) Make contracts, to such extent and in such amounts as are provided in appropriation acts, for the carrying out of any pretrial service functions.

(12) Perform such other functions as specified (Pretrial Services Act, Report No. 97-791).

STATE SYSTEMS

The state probation and parole systems differ in many ways. An accurate portrayal of their individual operations involves in-depth analysis within each state environment. While acknowledging the differences in the state systems, certain elements and problem areas are common to all. The following discussion will delineate some of the major differences between state systems as well as describe their similarities. Specific examples will be provided regarding one state's approach for purposes of illustration.

Overview of Organization and Operation

One of the significant differences in the organization of state probation systems concerns whether they are located under the state's executive or judicial branch. An argument in favor of placement within the executive branch is that offender services normally exist under executive authority and this will result in closer, more effective coordination. This position was favored by the President's Task Force on Corrections in 1973 (Report on Corrections). The Task Force noted the benefit of uniform standards and coordinated staff training.

Although parole boards, unlike probation agencies,

52

are by nature an executive responsibility, the structure
of the parole boards may differ. In most states, the
parole board administers an integrated probation and
parole agency. The American Correctional Association
(1971) identified four basic parole board structures:

(1) Those administering an integrated probation and
parole agency.
(2) Those administering the parole function only.
(3) Those that are a subordinate component of a
department which administers the correctional
institutions.
(4) Those that are part of an agency which administers the institutional and probation services.

The major duty of a parole board is to decide
whether parole is to be granted or denied. Once the
parolee is in the community the parole board must also
decide if parole should be revoked or continued.

The selection process of parole board members
varies. An American Correctional Association research
project (1975) surveyed the process by which various
jurisdictions appoint parole board members (Parole,
1975). The study found that in 40 of the 54
jurisdictions the appointing authorities are Governors;
in two jurisdictions Board Members are Civil Service
appointees; and in the remaining 12 jurisdictions members
are selected by a variety of methods, most including the
participation of Governors, but not exclusively. In the
federal system (U.S. Parole Commission) the President of
the United States appoints the commissioners with the
advice and consent of the Senate.

The number of parole board members also varies among
the states. The American Correctional Association study
found that board membership ranged from three to twelve
members. Most jurisdictions are relatively small, with
24 having five members and 16 with three members. The
U.S. Parole Commission has eight members.

A national survey of parole board members (Selection
for Parole, 1966) revealed that the items considered by
them to be most important in parole decisions were
related to the risk of violation. Table 12 indicates the
study results.

TABLE 12

ITEMS CONSIDERED BY PAROLE BOARD MEMBERS
TO BE MOST IMPORTANT IN PAROLE DECISIONS

Item	% Including Item as One of Five Most Important
1. My estimate of the chances that the prisoner would or would not commit a serious crime if paroled.	92.8
2. My judgment that the prisoner would benefit from further experience in the institution program or, at any rate, would become a better risk if confined longer.	87.1
3. My judgment that the prisoner would become a worse risk if confined longer.	71.9
4. My judgment that the prisoner had already been punished enough to "pay" for his crime.	43.2
5. The probability that the prisoner would be a misdemeanant and a burden to his parole supervisors, even if he did not commit any serious offenses on parole.	35.3
6. My feelings about how my decision in this case would affect the feelings or welfare of the prisoner's relatives or dependents.	33.8
7. What I thought the reaction of the judge might be if the prisoner were granted parole.	20.9

Source: National Parole Institutes, Selection for Parole (New York: NCCD, 1966).

Some state parole boards have responsibilities in addition to the granting of parole. Table 13 points out some of the additional responsibilities assumed by parole boards.

TABLE 13

RESPONSIBILITIES OF ADULT PAROLING AGENCIES
OTHER THAN PAROLE

Additional Responsibility	Number of Boards
Holds clemency hearings	28

(CHART 2 CONTINUED)

Commutes sentences	24
Appoints parole supervision staff	24
Administers parole service	20
Paroles from local institutions	19
Grants or withholds "good time"	17
Supervises probation service	14
Grants pardons, restorations, and remissions	1
Fixes maximum sentence after 6 months	1
May discharge prior to sentence expiration	1
Sets standards for "good time"	1
Acts as advisory board on pardons	1
None	5

Source: NCCD, Correction in the United States
         (New York: NCCD, 1967).

Budget

Unlike the budget of the federal probation system which is only a portion of the judicial budget, the overall budgets of the "hodge-podge" of state agencies cannot be so easily apportioned. Nevertheless, the United States Department of Justice has gathered valuable budgetary data by which comparisons might be made, including the expenditures for institutions and correctional administration. The figures reveal the proportionally small expenditures allotted to probation and parole functions (typically 10 percent), of the overall correctional budgets (see Table 14).

TABLE 14

EXPENDITURES FOR STATE CORRECTIONAL ACTIVITIES (1978)

Male Correctional Institutions:	$1,449,822,000
Female Correctional Institutions:	73,919,000
Juvenile Correctional Institutions:	505,363,000
Corrections Administration:	232,864,000
Probation, Parole, and Pardon:	348,290,000

Source: U.S. Department of Justice, LEAA, 1980.

The salaries of the probation and parole officers in the state settings are significantly less than those of federal probation officers. As Table 15 illustrates, the variation between states is also substantial.

TABLE 15

SALARY RANGE FOR STATE PROBATION AND PAROLE OFFICERS
BY JURISDICTION (AUGUST, 1979)

(Mean minimum salary:$12,204 / Mean maximum salary:$16,206)

Jurisdiction	Minimum Salary	Maximum Salary	Rank Based on Minimum Salary
Alabama................	$14,963	$17,472	4
Alaska.................	18,228	21,840	2
Arizona................	12,244	15,663	20
Arkansas...............	9,802	14,274	46
California.............	20,404	24,595	1
Colorado...............	12,600	16,896	17
Connecticut............	13,233	15,909	15
Delaware...............	10,757	14,521	40
Florida................	10,753	14,094	41
Georgia................	11,544	15,552	33
Hawaii.................	10,344	12,960	43
Idaho..................	11,040	14,796	38
Illinois...............	12,528	16,020	19
Indiana................	11,986	18,330	25
Iowa...................	13,790	17,950	11
Kansas.................	11,376	14,892	35
Kentucky...............	9,384	15,288	50
Louisiana..............	9,648	15,216	47
Maine..................	14,477	18,720	7
Maryland...............	10,231	13,340	44
Massachusetts..........	14,479	17,790	6
Michigan...............	13,989	14,511	10
Minnesota..............	13,238	16,391	14
Mississippi............	12,000	19,080	24
Missouri...............	11,148	14,448	37
Montana................	11,874	15,686	29
Nebraska...............	11,882	16,252	28
Nevada.................	12,058	16,504	22
New Hampshire..........	15,930	19,427	3
New Jersey.............	12,589	16,944	18
New Mexico.............	9,624	15,672	48

56

(TABLE 15 CONTINUED)

New York.............	14,850	18,780	5
North Carolina......	11,316	15,468	36
North Dakota........	12,108	17,040	21
Ohio................	11,980	15,579	26
Oklahoma............	11,940	15,840	27
Oregon..............	11,760	14,856	31
Pennsylvania........	13,666	17,714	13
Rhode Island........	14,411	16,997	8
South Carolina......	10,736	15,239	42
South Dakota........	11,826	17,722	30
Tennessee...........	10,152	13,536	45
Texas...............	13,692	17,244	12
Utah................	12,012	17,536	23
Vermont.............	10,920	17,290	39
Virginia............	11,472	15,675	34
Washington..........	11,748	14,976	32
West Virginia.......	9,504	15,516	49
Wisconsin...........	13,058	16,823	16
Wyoming.............	14,148	18,960	9
Puerto Rico.........	6,178	7,620	52
Virgin Islands......	8,966	11 ,215	51

Source: U.S.   Civil Service Commission, Bureau of Intergovernmental Personal Programs,   State   Salary
Survey, August 1, 1979.

_____

In   evaluating the comparative investments   made   by
the states to probation and parole functions per client,
Table 16 (under "Supervision") examines the recent indicators provided by ten southeastern states.   Notice the
comparatively low expenditures compared to the national
average, and the relatively wide range ($218 to $549).

Supervision

Many probation and parole officers have contended
for years that supervision of their cases would improve
if their caseloads were reduced in number.   Some feel
that an ideal caseload should not exceed 50 clients.   The
San Francisco Project (1969) studied the issue   of
caseload   size.   Four   levels   of   workloads   were
established: (1)   ideal   (50   cases);   (2) intensive
(25, half the ideal);   (3) normal (100, twice   the
ideal);   and (4) minimum supervision (with a ceiling of
250 cases).   As part of the study, persons in minimum
supervision caseloads were required only to submit a
monthly written report;   no contacts occurred except when

requested by the probationer. It was found that offenders in minimum caseloads performed as well as those under normal supervision. The minimum and ideal caseloads had almost identical violation rates. In the intensive caseloads, the violation rate did not decline, but technical violations increased.

The San Francisco Project suggested that the number of contacts between probationer and staff had little relationship to success or failure on probation. The study concluded that the concept of a caseload is meaningless without some type of classification and matching of offender type with service to be offered, and effective staffing to accomplish the goal.

Probation and parole officers across the United States must also work together in the supervision of probationers and parolees. Clegg (1970) reported that states entered into agreements (compacts) for supervision of parolees and probationers, beginning with the passage of the Inter-State Parole and Probation Compact in 1934. Compacts permit parolees and probationers to return to their home residence and still be under proper supervision by local probation and parole authorities.

Clegg (1970) also observed that the Inter-State Compact accomplished two objectives:

(1) It protected the community by providing supervision for the offender.

(2) It increased the chances of successful reformation for the offender by permitting his return to a locality where he had a family, acquaintances, and job opportunities.

TABLE 16

COMPARATIVE SUPERVISION INDICATORS AND EXPENDITURES FOR TEN SOUTHEASTERN STATES AND THE UNITED STATES (1982)

State	Rate of Supervision per 100,000 Adults	Average Caseload	Expense per Supervision Client
Alabama	572	154	$258

(TABLE 16 CONTINUED)

Florida	735	66	494
Georgia	1408	100	320
Louisiana	614	79	549
Mississippi	500	110	262
North Carolina	1127	105	349
South Carolina	811	110	350
Tennessee	409	105	469
Texas	1342	113	384
Virginia	459	59	525
U.S.(states only)	831	64	877
U.S.(fed. included)	870	59	---

Source: S.C. Parole and Community Corrections,1982.

Investigation

The major duties of parole and probation officers include investigation as well as supervision. Some officers have a difficult time with the dual functions. How can an officer be a "helper" on the one hand and a "watch-dog" on the other? Ohlin, Piven, and Pappenfort (1956) made a study of probation officers and their work roles. They determined that three work orientation types were prevalent: (1) the "punitive officer," (2) the "protective agent," and (3) the "welfare worker."

The punitive officer assumes that he or she is the protector of middle class values, with a duty to protect society from his or her clients. The protective agent is ambivalent. He is protective of both community and client. The officer's reaction (e.g., praise or rejection) depends on the prevailing circumstances, not his or her basic value preferences. The welfare worker, on the other hand, is oriented toward the client. This officer goes out of the way to meet the needs of the probationer or parolee.

The accompanying Table 17 reveals both the large number of cases requiring supervision in the states, and also the large number of presentence investigations. It should be noted, however, that approximately 12 of the 50 states do not regularly perform presentence investigations. The failure to undertake presentence investigations usually reflects a probation and parole authority that is lacking in necessary resources, or a judiciary that is resistant to change.

TABLE 17

SUPERVISION CASES AND PRESENTENCE REPORTS
COMPLETED NATIONALLY (1978)

CASES SUPERVISED

	Federal	State	Total
Conditional Release	21,491	123,621	145,112
Interstate Compact	0	32,976	32,976
Probation	45,472	292,523	337,995
Other	2,317	12,159	14,476
Total	69,280	415,284	484,564

PRESENTENCE REPORTS COMPLETED

Federal	State	Total
26,403	145,300	171,703

Source: National Council on Crime and Delinquency, Parole in the United States: 1978, pp. 32,33.

Revocation

The requirements of the revocation process may differ among the states. The due process and procedural safeguards mandated by recent judicial decisions, however, are applicable to both the federal and state system. The previously mentioned Morrissey case is a prime example of a landmark judicial decision requiring modification of existing state procedures.

The revocation of parole by a parole authority has been traditionally justified on three theoretical grounds: The Privilege theory; The Contract Theory; and The Continuing Custody Theory (Palmer, 1973). the Privilege Theory considers parole to be within the total discretion of the state, thus a privilege. Such an approach appears to ignore the realities of parole's importance and prevalence within the criminal justice system. The Contract Theory views parole as an agreement between two contracting parties, the violation of which subjects the violator to the penalties provided. The logic of this rationale, however, is somewhat strained, as the relationship of the contracting parties is hardly equal or voluntary in nature. Finally, the Continuing Custody Theory considers parole only as an extension of the confinement process, thus subject to the same restrictions. This theory of treating parolees as inmates is also faulty in that the freedoms enjoyed by each are not truly comparable. As evidenced by recent judicial decisions, the courts have been unwilling to embrace any single theory of parole, and have severely limited the application of each through imposition of due process requirements. This had led to a recognition of a fourth theory by some observers, understandably referred to as the Due Process Theory, which reflects recent judicial decisions and legal mandates.

The majority of parolees are discharged from their parole conditions by completing their terms or by obtaining early discharges. Table 18 illustrates the types and incidences of removal experienced by all states during 1979.

TABLE 18

PAROLE REMOVALS (1979)

1)	Completion of Term	59.2%
2)	Revocation or Recommitment	24.8%
3)	Early Discharge	10.3%
4)	Other (e.g., Death)	5.7%

Source: U.S. Department of Justice, Parole In The United States, 1980.

Pretrial Services

State pretrial service programs, like those of the

federal system, permit intervention into a case before it comes to court. Frequently, the defendant enters a program of counseling and guidance, since supervised pretrial programs generally offer rehabilitation or treatment for eligible defendants, especially those charged with non-violent crimes. Restitution to the victim is also sometimes required of participants. States exercise substantial latitude in their individual programs, but the following requirements (South Carolina Pretrial Intervention Program, 1983) may be considered typical of those imposed on defendants:

> Program requirements differ from charge to charge and from defendant to defendant. There are, however, several ground rules. All defendants are assigned a counselor and are responsible for making contact with him for a duration of a minimum of 90 days and a maximum of one year. The defendant is required to attend an organized tour of a correctional facility, perform a minimum of 15 hours volunteer work, and seek meaningful employment. Defendants who have special needs or problems may be referred, on a contract basis, by their counselors to other agencies such as Alcohol and Drug Abuse, Mental Health, Vocational Rehabilitation, Technical Education, Department of Social Services, etc. In cases where it is appropriate to compensate victims for their losses, restitution is required from the defendant before he can complete the diversion program (South Carolina Pretrial Intervention Report, 1983).

The factors leading to the increased emphasis on state pretrial services are numerous. The programs are often self-supporting due to the funding by participants. Since many of the programs require restitution, direct benefits accrue to the victims. Other advantages may include: (a) immediate treatment and counseling; (b) criminal record avoidance; (c) vocational training; (d) reduced prison populations; and (e) relief to taxpayers. In summary, the numerous and substantial benefits of pretrial services are compelling, whenever appropriate.

References

Administrative Office of the United States Courts. (1980)
 1980 annual report of the director. Washington,
 DC: U.S. Government Printing Office.

Administrative Office of the United States Courts. (1981)
 1981 annual report of the director. Washington,DC:
 U.S. Government Printing Office.

Administrative Office of the United States Courts. (1980)
 Federal judicial workload statistics. Washington,DC:
 U.S. Government Printing Office.

Administrative Office of the United States Courts.(1976).
 *Report on the implementation of title I and title II
 of the Speedy Trial Act of 1974*. Washington, DC:
 U.S.Government Printing Office.

Administrative Office of the United States Courts. (1981)
 Speedy Trial Act of 1974. Washington, DC: U.S.
 Government Printing Office.

American Correctional Association. (1971). *Manual of
 correctional standards*.

Bureau of the Census, National Criminal Justice Information and Statistics Service. (1978). *State and local
 probation and parole systems*. Washington, DC: U.S.
 Government Printing Office.

Clegg, R.K. *Probation and parole*. (1970). Charles C.
 Thomas Publisher.

Federal Judicial Center. (1976). *An introduction to
 the federal probation system*. Washington, DC:
 Author.

Gagnon v. Scarpelli. 411 U.S. 471 (1973).

Morrissey v. Brewer. 408 U.S. 471 (1972).

National Advisory Commission on Criminal Justice
 Standards and Goals. (1973). *Report on corrections*.
 Washington, D.C.: U.S. Government Printing Office.

National Parole Institutes. (1966). *Selection for
 parole*. New York: National Council on Crime and
 Delinquency.

Ohlin, L.E., Piven, H. & Pappenfort, D.M. (1956). Major dilemmas of the social worker in probation and parole. NPPA Journal, 2 (3), 215.

Palmer, J.W. (1977). Constitutional rights of prisoners. Cincinnati: Anderson.

Parker, W.C. (1975) Parole. College Park, MD: American Correctional Association.

Prus, R.C. & Stratton, J.R. (1976). Parole revocation decisionmaking: private typings and official designations. Federal Probation, March.

Reports of the proceedings of the judicial conference of the United States. (1980). Washington, DC.

Robinson, J. et al. (1969). The San Francisco project. Berkeley, CA: University of California School of Criminology.

Ryan, D.B. (1977). The federal pretrial services agencies. Federal Probation, March, 15-22.

United States Courts. (1976). Pretrial services. Washington, DC: U.S. Government Printing Office.

United States 93rd Congress. Speedy Trial Act of 1974. Public Law 93-619, Section 18 U.S. Code 3152.

United States 93rd Congress. Speedy Trial Act of 1974. Public Law 93-619, Section 18 U.S. Code 3153 (b).

United States Department of Justice. (1980) Parole in the United States. Washington, DC: U.S. Government Printing Office.

United States Department of Justice. (1980). Sourcebook of criminal justice statistics. Washington, DC: U.S. Government Printing Office.

Chapter 4

PROBATION AND PAROLE OFFICERS: DUTIES AND RESPONSIBILITIES

LEARNING OBJECTIVES

* Understand the operations of effective case management.

* Knowledge of the importance and substance of presentence investigations.

* Learning the requirements of proper client supervision.

* Developing strategies for providing client treatment and referrals.

DISCUSSION QUESTIONS

1. What is a Client Management Classification (CMC) System and how does it operate?

2. What are the important elements of presentence investigations?

3. How does a probation or parole officer determine the appropriate form of supervision? What type of conditions may be imposed on the client?

4. Why are treatment and referral programs important? How may a probation or parole officer become aware of treatment and referral alternatives?

CASE MANAGEMENT

Modern case management is increasingly being utilized through the implementation of new Client Management Classification (CMC) Systems. CMC Systems are designed to meet two specific needs. First, these systems are designed to help in management by determining the level of surveillance that should be employed in each probation/parole case (National Advisory Commission, 1973). A second purpose is that of determining client needs as well as identifying resources to meet them. This second concern is not of recent origin, but was a concern for some of the earliest students of criminology, including Lombroso, Ferri and Garofalo (Schafer, 1969). Classification processes continue to receive much attention in the corrections setting, where classification schemes are critical to both inmate assignments and institutional priorities (Abadinsky, 1983).

In recent years, newly designed client management classification models have been developed to meet both the needs of caseload management and client classification. The most elaborate and successful model to date has been the Client Management Classification System (CMC), first developed and utilized in Wisconsin in 1975, and adopted by the National Institute of Corrections (NIC Draft Report, 1983).

The NIC has embraced CMC as a pragmatic and easily administered classification and case handling approach for adult probation or parole clients (NIC, 1983). The procedures incorporated within CMC assist officers in three ways: (1) gaining a quick appreciation and understanding of the client's problems and needs; (2) identifying impediments to solving the client's problems; and (3) developing an appropriate and effective casework plan.

The CMC is employed at the earliest intake phase, enabling clients to be assigned to casework groups based upon an empirically scored, structured interview--a device that saves time and assists in developing coherent treatment strategies. Early evaluations of the CMC have documented its accuracy in classifying clients, its effectiveness in saving time and resources, and its desirability by probation and parole officers implementing it.

The Client Management Classification System is comprised of four specific treatment modalities: (1) Selective Intervention; (2) Environmental Structure; (3) Casework/Control; and (4) Limit Settings. These labels identify the characteristic supervision strategy to be employed with each group, and serve as a framework for developing a client relationship. A brief description of each modality follows:

1. Selective Intervention. This group is designed for clients who enjoy relatively stable and pro-social life-styles (e.g. employed, established in community, and minimal criminal records). Such offenders have typically experienced an isolated and stressful event, or neurotic problem. With effective intervention, there is a higher chance of avoiding future difficulty. The goals of treatment for these individuals include the development of appropriate responses to temporary crises and problems, and the re-establishment of pro-life patterns.

2. Environmental Structure. The dominant character-istics of clients in this group consist of deficiencies in social, vocational, and intellectual skills. Most of their problems stem from their inability to succeed in their employment or to be comfortable in most social settings--an overall lack of social skills and intellectual cultivation/ability. The goals for these clients include: (a) developing basic employment and social skills; (b) selecting alternatives to association with criminally-oriented peers; and (c) improving social skills and impulse controls.

3. Casework/Control. This group of clients manifests instabilities in their lives as evidenced by failures in employment and domestic problems. A lack of goal-directedness is present, typically associated with alcohol and drug problems. Offense patterns include numerous arrests, although marketable job skills are present. Unstable childhoods, family pressure, and financial difficulties are typically present. The goals appropriate for this group include promoting stability in their professional and domestic endeavors, and achieving an improved utilization of the individual's potential along with an elimination of self-defeating behavior and emotional/psychological problems.

4. <u>Limit Setting</u>. Clients in this group are commonly considered to be successful and career criminals because of their long-term involvement in criminal activities. They generally enjoy "beating the system," they frequently act for material gain, and they show little remorse or guilt. Because of their value system, they easily adapt to prison environments and return to crime upon release. Goals for the group are problematic, but include changing the client's basic attitudes and closely supervising their behavior within the community.

CMC utilizes the above categories by placing the client into the proper modality based upon a structured interview of less than one hour. Upon classification, an individualized treatment plan is developed based on the following guidelines (NIC Draft Report, 1983): (a) General description of clients; (b) Suggested treatment goals; (c) Anticipated client-agent relationship (positive and negative); (d) Auxiliary referral sources likely to be used; and (e) Suggested techniques for approaching clients in each group.

Early results of this plan in Wisconsin found that clients generally were classified in each mode in the following manner: (1) Selective Intervention treatment (40%); (2) Environmental Structure model (15%); (3) Casework Control mode (30%); and (4) Limit Setting group (15%). Some states (e.g., South Carolina) are presently in the initial stages of implementing this program and results are, as yet, unknown.

In conclusion, the CMC seems to offer the following advantages to adult probation and parole agents: (a) effective and simplified intake interviewing procedures; (b) systematic methods for integrating information regarding client needs; (c) the formulation of in-depth case plans; and (d) an objective basis for classifying and managing client programs, free of individual and hidden bias. In addition, advantages accruing to probation and parole agencies are likely to include (a) the assignment of cases based upon agents' skills and preferences; (b) the creation of higher expectations among supervisors by promoting increased training, better strategies and a basis for evaluating performance; and (c) the production of better trained and more knowledgeable agents, capable of dealing more productively with client needs.

PRESENTENCE INVESTIGATION

Presentence investigations (PSI's) comprise the primary investigative duties of most probation officers. As previously indicated, however, some states do not utilize presentence investigations to their full potential. One system which does place heavy reliance upon these reports is the federal probation system. Because of the high degree of professionalization and funding of the United States Probation Office, it will serve as a model for describing the potential for utilization of presentence investigations.

The basic duties and responsibilities of federal probation officers stem from four sources: (1) statutes; (2) Federal rules; (3) court directives; and (4) administrative agreements. The pertinent statutes related to the duties of a probation officer are found in Title 18 of the United States Code. For example, Section 3655 requires the probation officer to furnish each probationer a copy of his or her probation conditions, and supervise and monitor the probationer's compliance. The Federal Rules of Criminal Procedure impose responsibilities on probation officers. For example, Rule 32 (c)(1) requires the probation officer to supply the court with a presentence report prior to imposing a sentence, unless otherwise directed. Court directives are also important to the probation officer. The U. S. Code, section 3401 (c) specifically provides that a U. S. Magistrate may request investigation reports, upon the approval of a Federal District Court Judge. Finally, some duties of the probation officer are derived from administrative agreement. These agreements promote cooperation and greater efficiency between agencies which may somtimes have overlapping responsibilities, such as the Bureau of Prisons and the armed services. As a result, Federal Probation Officers must be knowledgeable of specific and unique responsibilities in addition to those related to the community.

Presentence Investigations required of a federal probation officer include:

(a) Presentence Investigation Reports (which are written reports to assist the court in disposing of criminal cases);
(b) Selective Presentence Investigations (which are generally used in misdemeanor cases);

(c) Collateral Investigation Reports (which are prepared in districts other than the district in which final dispositions of the cases are made);

(d) Preliminary Investigation Reports (which assist United States Attorneys in determining whether the cases of alleged offenders should be diverted or deferred);

(e) Postsentence Investigation Reports (which are completed after the disposition of cases.

An individual undergoing a presentence investigation is instructed by the probation officer to bring important information and selected papers to assist in the presentence investigation. These papers help in the verification of facts reported to the probation officer. The following items are frequently requested by probation officers:

Birth/baptismal certificate
School diplomas
Proof of residence (rent receipts, etc.)
Draft registration card
Military discharge papers
Military disability information (C-number)
Seaman's papers
Marriage certificate
Divorce decree
Social Security number
Department of Welfare records

Income tax reports for last three years
Employment verification (pay stubs)
Union/lodge/club cards
Immigration papers or or passport
Naturalization papers
Professional papers (licenses or permits)
Car registration papers
Medical reports (if presently under doctor's care)

The accompanying illustrations of authorization demonstrate how a defendant must sign a release to the government and private persons and organizations regarding information pertinent to the presentence investigation.

ILLUSTRATION 1

AUTHORIZATION TO RELEASE GOVERNMENT
(STATE OR FEDERAL) INFORMATION TO PROBATION OFFICER

I,_____, the undersigned, hereby waive my rights under the Privacy Act, 5 U.S.C. 552a (Supp. IV, 1974), and authorize the disclosure to the United States Probation Office of the _____District of _____, or its authorized representative(s) or employee(s), any and all information pertaining to me, contained in the files or systems of records maintained by any government agency subject to the Privacy Act, which such agency sees fit to convey, either orally or in writing, to the aforementioned Probation Office.

I hereby waive any rights I may have under the Privacy Act to prior notice of such disclosure or of any rights I may have to an accounting of such disclosure to the aforementioned Probation Office.

I understand that this consent will be used by the aforementioned Probation Office to request disclosure of information pertaining to me from any or all Federal agencies.

This information is to be obtained for the purpose of conducting a presentence investigation and making a report of for supervision.

---

authorizing signature	full name	date

parent/guardian
sig.,if required

attorney sig., if
available

WITNESS-

probation officer   date

ILLUSTRATION 2

AUTHORIZATION TO RELEASE INFORMATION
(PRIVATE PERSON OR ORGANIZATION) TO PROBATION
OFFICER

TO WHOM IT MAY CONCERN:

I,_____, the undersigned, hereby
authorize the United States Probation Office for
the _____ District of_____
or its authorized representative(s) or employee(s),
bearing this release or copy thereof, to obtain any
information in your files pertaining to my
employment; credit or educational records including
but not limited to academic, achievement,
attendance, athletic, personal history, and
disciplinary records; medical records; and credit
records. I hereby direct you to release such
information upon request of the bearer. This
release is executed with full knowledge and
understanding that the information is for the
official use of the aforementioned United States
Probation Office.

I hereby release you, as custodian of such
records; any school, college, university, or other
educational institution; hospital or other
repository of medical records; credit bureau;
lending institution; consumer reporting agency; or
retail business establishment including its
officers, employees, or related personnel, both
individually and collectively, from any and all
liability for damages of whatever kind which may at
any time result to me, my heirs, family, or
associates because of compliance with this
authorization and request for information or any
other attempt to comply with it.

The information hereby obtained by the
aforementioned Probation Office is to be used for
the purpose of presentence investigation and report
or for supervision.

_____   _____ _____
authorizing signature   full name   date

WITNESS-   _____ _____
                                 probation officer   date

The presentence report is the basic working document for the Federal Probation Service and the courts as well. It is usually the most detailed and comprehensive report, serving the following five purposes: (a) assisting the court in deciding upon appropriate sentences; (b) guiding the probation officer in matters of supervision; (c) assisting prison officials in classifying and treating offenders; (d) aiding in the consideration of parole; and (e) providing valuable information for statistical and research purposes. From these reports, valuable information is developed which provides an insight into the character and personality of the defendant and also the defendant's special problems or needs. The report demonstrates the defendant's social circumstances, relationships with people and other information which helps to reveal the nature of his or her offense and general conduct.

The following discussion will outline the proper preparation of the PSI, describing the report's important details. In illustrating the report, refer to the hypothetical presentence investigation of client John Doe in the exercise section of the text.

An interview process must be undertaken by the probation officer prior to completion of a PSI report. During the interview process, the Federal Probation Officer must gather special information about the defendant--his or her background and other pertinent facts--which will assist in the completion of the PSI Report. This information is detailed in the accompanying exercises following the text.

The face sheet of the PSI requires numerous items of basic information. In the Plea/Verdict section, indicate the count(s) to which the defendant either pled or was found guilty. In the Custody section, note the date that the defendant was released on bond, or how long he or she has remained in confinement. Regarding codefendants, mention, if possible, what sentences they received and the sentencing judge. Regarding Detainers or Warrants pending, briefly spell out what the charges are, the jurisdiction, and the next hearing date.

The presentence investigation report must detail the following twelve items of information:

(I)   OFFENSE:

The   "Who, What, When, How and Where"   of newspaper parlance would seem to be applicable here.   Be brief, but indicate the specifics of the charge, such as the location and time of the official version of the offense. Although not really essential to the official version of the offense, it is important to note supplemental information (e.g., the current condition of any victim, the recovery of property, the nature of the drug offense).

(II)   DEFENDANT'S VERSION OF OFFENSE:

Here one should first obtain the defendant's side of the story, and then ascertain any discrepancies between the official version and his/her version. In addition, questions concerning why the defendant was at the scene of the crime, or what type of weapon was used, may be appropriate. Finally, and obviously most important, does he/she now admit the offense (even though the offender may have denied the charges at the trial). If a plea of guilty was entered, does the defendant now contend that he/she did not commit the offense. As a final point, the probation officer should ask these and other questions in an appropriate manner in order to gain the most accurate and relevant information from the defendant.

(III)   PRIOR ARREST RECORD:

Entries should be noted chronologically, beginning with the earliest arrest. If the charges are serious, or the defendant received a sentence or probation for them, one should attempt to get some official statements regarding the charges and obtain the defendant's comments regarding the arrests. If probation was granted, some attempt should be made to determine how the defendant behaved while under probation supervision. If the defendant has been arrested on new charges while out on bond in the current case, one should detail this in the presentence report, and try to get information regarding the offense. If possible, schedule a definite hearing date.

(IV)   PERSONAL AND FAMILY DATA:

Here the aim is simply to indicate to the Court, without a great deal of unnecessary information, what might be termed a "Social History." Specifically include: (a) date and place of birth; (b) who reared the defendant, whether his/her home was intact; (c) defendant's relationships with family and their comments about the defendant (through an interview); (d) when the defendant left home and what he/she has been engaged in since. NOTE: Obviously the older the defendant, the less emphasis one would place on a discussion of his/her "formative" years. If any of the family members impress you as concerned about the defendant, and comment on what they believe are the reasons for his/her getting involved in the offense, then you should so indicate. Also, it is very important that one determine whether any of the family members could be considered a resource for the defendant should the Court decide to utilize probation.

(V)   MARITAL HISTORY:

Numerous important items of information should be covered here, including: (a) date and place (along with wife's/husband's name) of marriage, along with verification, if possible; (b) whether marriage is "meretricious" or common law, along with such information as how long couple has been living together, number and ages of children, whether the children are with them; (c) the number and ages of any children born out of wedlock, the name of the mother/father of the children, where the children are, whether the defendant is providing for their support, and if defendant is under court order to do so; and (d) if the defendant claims to have a girlfriend/boyfriend, and whether he/she plans to marry soon or not. NOTE: An interview with the defendant's wife, husband, common law partner, or girlfriend/boy-friend is very important.

(VI)   EDUCATION:

Here one should note how much education the defendant claims, any "special" training he/she may have received, and what basic level of intellect the defendant appears to have (i.e., below average intelligence, boderline, average, superior, etc.). Also if a relatively young defendant, it might be helpful to the court if his/her I.Q. is determined.

(VII)   HEALTH:

This section can be very important or routine, depending on the defendant and the offense. Generally, a simple statement that "the defendant states that his present mental and physical health is satisfactory," will suffice. If he/she denies the excessive use of alcohol, or claims that he/she has never taken what might be considered narcotics in any form (including the smoking of marijuana), the statements themselves will be helpful. However, if one detects the possibility of a history of mental or emotional illness, or the defendant is before the Court on a drug charge and admits to the use of narcotics, or other unusual conditions are present, more information must be provided. NOTE: The official policy is generally to obtain a urine sample (which is tested) on all drug cases and on all defendants (whether a drug case or not) who have a history of drug abuse.

(VIII) EMPLOYMENT:

This section should begin with the defendant's present employment status. List the most current employment, month and year of claimed employment, the name and address of the firm, the position held and claimed salary (see Illustration 3).

ILLUSTRATION 3

DEFENDANT'S WORK HISTORY

(1) Current employment:
6-78 to date of arrest.   Ace Wrecking Co.   Laborer
                           1215 Va. Av.,NE
                           City
                           $210 per week

Information verified that the defendant was considered an "excellent worker" and that the company would rehire the defendant if probation is granted.

(2) Past employment:
5-77 to 5-78. During this period the defendant states that he held a number of short-term jobs as a day laborer, none for longer than a few days at a time. He was usually paid around $3.25 an hour.

4-75 to 4-77. The defendant candidly admitted that he held no salaried employment at all during this time, stating that he supported himself by "hustling," gambling, and from the proceeds of the sale of various merchandise which he shoplifted from area department stores.

7-71 to 3-77. In custody at the U.S. Penitentiary, Atlanta, Georgia during this period, serving a 3-9 year term for manslaughter (see PRIOR ARREST RECORD).

(IX):   MILITARY:

This section is not as determinative as it once was. However, if the defendant has had military service, it should be noted (e.g., branch, dates of service, type of discharge, any AWOL and other disciplinary charges, or anytime served in confinement). If he/she is within the required age range, it should be noted wheter he or she registered for the draft.

(X)   FINANCIAL CONDITION:

The importance and necessity for data here will, as with some of the other sections of the report, depend on the defendant, his/her background and the nature of the offense. If the offender is an income tax violater, stock manipulator or involved in a complex fraud case, for instance, it may be necessary to have the defendant submit an itemized "statement of net worth." If the defendant is young, with no obvious resources, this section can be handled simply by indicating what he/she claims in the way of assets and liabilities.

(XI)   EVALUATIVE SUMMARY:

This section will probably be considered the most important part of your report, for it is here that one should be able to: (a) develop a profile of the defendant for the court; (b) bring together in some meaningful manner all of the historic and other data that has previously been reported; (c) give the court some possible reasons for the defendant's involvement, what his/her strengths and weaknesses are, and the personal impression the defendant gives; (d) indicate whether the defendant appears to be a good probation risk or might pose a threat to the community, with reasons to support the conclusions. (NOTE: It is not necessary or desirable to simply repeat what has been previously stated in the report. On the contrary, two or three paragraphs of evaluation, diagnosis and prognosis would appear to be all that is necessary.)

(XII)   RECOMMENDATION:

The recommendation should be typed on a separate page. If the report has been prepared properly, the recommendation for or against the use of probation should be obvious. If probation is recommended, one should indicate any special conditions of probation that you feel will be called for, such as restitution, particiaption in drug aftercare program, involvement with

Alcoholics Anonymous, along with a tentative plan of
treatment (which will not necessarily be considered
specific conditions of probation (see Illustration 4).

ILLUSTRATION 4

SUPERVISION PLAN

Should the Court concur with this recommendation for
probation, the following, tentative community plan has
been developed for the defendant:

(a) Residence: Will return to the home of his
parents at 1102 First Street, SW, for now at least.
(b) Employment: Arrangements will be made to
assist the defendant with a job through the Employment
Counseling Services Division of the D.C. Government. We
will also explore with this agency the possibilty of
securing a program of trade training for the defendant as
a computer technician.
(c) Other: For at least the first six months of
his probation supervision, the defendant has agreed to
attend and participate in our office's weekly group counseling program where the emphasis in working with him
will be on job counseling.

It should be noted that Rule 32 (c)(3) of the
Federal Rules of Criminal Procedure allows a federal
judge to exclude certain information from review by an
offender and his attorney. For instance, a psychological
report, if read by a defendant, might interfere with his
future prospects for rehabilitation. Generally, however,
a defendant and his attorney may be permitted to read a
presentence investigation report except for the sentence
recommendation page which is for the judge only.

CLIENT SUPERVISION

Supervision of a client is a fundamental task in
which a probation/parole officer (PO) should become
proficient. Since interviews and on-site visits are
essential activities, proper supervision generally
requires a command of various counseling techniques. The
PO must be able to assist the probationer/parolee in the
development of social skills and in problem-solving.
Frequently the officer must gather information from the
client's employer, associates, and relatives. He or she
must also establish and maintain accurate case files,
which include data on his/her treatment, attitudes, and

behavior. In addition, the accuracy and availability of these records becomes especially important when a probationer or parolee changes jurisdiction, or when research data are needed.

When a person has been placed on probation or parole, one of the first steps an officer takes is to read and explain the conditions of supervision. Typical conditions are included in the federal conditions of probation (see Illustration 5).

ILLUSTRATION 5

CONDITIONS OF PROBATION FOR THE U.S. DISTRICT COURT

It is the order of the Court that you shall comply with the following conditions of probation:

(1) You shall refrain from violation of any law (federal, state, and local). You shall get in touch immediately with your probation officer if arrested or questioned by a law-enforcement officer.
(2) You shall associate only with law-abiding persons and maintain reasonable hours.
(3) You shall work regularly at a lawful occupation and support your legal dependents, if any, to the best of your ability. When out of work you shall notify your probation officer at once. You shall consult with him prior to job changes.
(4) You shall not leave the judicial district without permission of the probation officer.
(5) You shall notify your probation officer immediately of any change in your place of residence.
(6) You shall follow the probation officer's instructions.
(7) You shall report to the PO as directed.

It is required that each individual under supervision submit written reports as ordered by the court. Each individual completes the forms and submits them by a designated time period, usually each month. If a probationer or parolee desires to travel to a different jurisdiction, he/she must complete a permission to travel form. This form protects the probationer or parolee if he/she is questioned by law enforcement officials about his/her presence in their jurisdiction.

A federal probation officer generally uses a Risk Prediction Scale (RPS 80) on a new probationer to determine what type of supervision is needed. A new federal parolee has a similar scale, the Salient Factor Score, (SFS), which determines if the supervision level should be low or high activity.

Using the risk score, the probation officer determines a level of supervision. In some cases there are circumstances where the probation officer may need to increase the level of supervision. During the initial six months of supervision the supervision level is not to be less than what the predictive device indicates (Administrative Office of the U.S. Courts, 1981).

There are two basic levels of supervision, low activity and high activity. The purpose and value of differentially designating persons to one of these two levels is to free the probation officer to direct systematically his/her skills and energies to those in greatest need of services and monitoring. Persons in the low activity supervision level, as reflected in their histories, have usually experienced relative success in establishing personal stability. Although occasionally it is necessary for the probation officer to respond to crisis situations, sustained contact is seldom necessary. The PO attempts to manage these cases through the use of referred services and collateral contacts. The PO should not encourage more than one personal contact per quarter and three personal contacts per quarter should be the exception rather than the rule. Persons in the high activity supervision level have usually experienced difficulty in establishing and maintaining personal stability. The PO should direct the greatest effort toward persons in the high activity supervision level. There is no upper limit on the number of times a given person may be seen in a month's time. All persons in this supervision level, however, are to be seen at least once a month. The purpose, frequency, and location of personal and collateral contacts are shaped by the supervision plan. Once a new probationer has been rated by the RPS 80 scale, a classification and initial supervision plan is designed.

A case review is completed by a PO after a client has been under supervision for a period of time. The case review explains the progress or lack of progress made by a client during a certain period of time. The PO also keeps a chronological record of the activities of the client. This chronological record points out the dates the client reported to the office and what problems he/she has faced during the period of supervision. The PO similarly keeps a travel record to plan out his/her day in the field. The record lists the individuals he/she visited and the cases which were investigated. The field sheet of the PO gives address and employment information on a client. The PO keeps an accurate record of contacts on a record of reports/visits form.

TREATMENT AND REFERRALS

The PO must develop helpful strategies to deal with problem areas of a probationer or parolee's life. Problems can range from drug abuse to employment difficulties. If the problems facing a probationer or parolee need the assistance of a specialist, a referral is required. A recent major study revealed a positive association between receiving services and success on probation (State and County Probation: Systems in Crisis, 1976). The report recommended that departments try to provide clients with as many of the needed services as possible.

Many probationers and parolees need intensive supervision which may be provided by residence in a halfway house. A judge or a parole board can require offenders to live in a halfway house as a condition of their release. A national study by Donald Thalheime (1975) pointed out the following goals for halfway houses: (a) development of attributes conducive to good employment; (b) placing the inmate in employment which he or she may retain after release; (c) providing an atmosphere suitable for education; (d) reducing confinements to state institutions; and (e) offering an effective residential program at less cost per offender than institutions.

A PO often finds that a client with a drinking problem should be referred to Alcoholics Anonymous (AA). This organization was founded in Akron, Ohio in 1935 (The Society of Alcoholics Anonymous, 1949). AA members meet on a regular basis to hear testimonials from individuals who have successfully abstained from drinking. The AA group reinforces the probationer or parolee that he/she is not alone in their struggle with alcohol dependency.

Drug usage other than alcohol is a related major problem for offenders. Carney (1977) reports that up to 25% of all crime is drug related. The probation officer must seek out innovative programs to deal with this problem and obtain client participation.

The probation officer sometimes also has to learn the slang terms that are associated with drug usage. The Bureau of Narcotics and Dangerous Drugs (1971) published the following guide to assist criminal justice personnel who work on drug investigations (see Illustration 6).

ILLUSTRATION 6

IMPORTANT TERMS FOR EFFECTIVE DRUG ENFORCEMENT

Official Names	Slang Terms
Marihuana	Smoke, straw, Texas tea, jive, pod, mutah, splim, Acapulco Gold, Bhang, boo, bush, butter flower, Ganja, weed, grass, pot, muggles, tea, hash, hemp, griffo, Indian hay, loco weed, hay, herb, J, mu, giggles-smoke, love weed, Mary Warner, Mohasky, Mary Jane, joint sticks, reefers, sativa, roach
Amphetamines	Pep pills, bennies, wake-ups, eye-openers, lid poppers, co-pilots, truck drivers, peaches, roses, hearts, cartwheels, whites, coast to coast, LA turnabouts, browns, footballs, greenies, bombido, oranges, dexies, jolly-beans, A's, jellie babies, sweets, beans, uppers
Morphine	M, dreamer, white stuff, hard stuff, morpho, unkie, Miss Emma, monkey, cube, morf, tab, emsel, hocus, morphie, melter
Codeine	Schoolboy
Heroin	Snow, stuff, H, junk, big Harry, caballo, DooJee, boy, horse, white stuff, Harry, hairy, joy powder, salt, dope, duige, hard stuff, smack, shit, skag, thing
Hydromorphone	Dilaudid, Lords

Meperidine	Demerol, Isonipecaine, Dolantol, Pethidine
Methadone	Dolophine, Dollies, dolls, amidone
Exempt Preparations	P.G., P.O., blue velvet (Paregoric with antihistamine), red water, bitter, licorice
Cocaine	The leaf, snow, C, cecil, coke, dynamite, flake, speedball (when mixed with Heroin), girl, happy dust, joy powder, white girl, gold dust, Corine, Bernies, Burese, gin, Bernice, Star dust, Carrie, Cholly, heaven dust, paradise
Methamphetamine	Speed, meth, splash, crystal, bombita, Methedrine, Doe
Other Stimulants	Pep pills, uppers
Barbiturates	Yellows, yellow jackets, nimby, nimbles, reds, pinks, red birds, red devils, seggy, seccy, pink ladies, blues, blue birds, blue devils, blue heavens, red & blues, double trouble, tooies, Christmas trees, phennies, barbs
Other Depressants	Candy, goofballs, sleeping pills, peanuts
LSD Lysergic Acid	Acid, cubes, pearly gates, heavenly blue, royal blue, wedding bells, sugar, Big D, Blue acid, the Chief, the Hawk, instant Zen, 25, Zen, sugar lump

STP	Serenity, tranquility, peace, DOM, syndicate acid
Phencyclidine (PCP)	PCP, peace pill, synthetic marihuana
Peyote	Mescal button, mescal beans, hikori, hikuli, huatari, seni, wokomi, cactus, the button, tops, a moon, half moon, P, the bad seed, Big Chief, Mesc
Psilocybin	Sacred mushrooms, mushroom
Dimethltryptamine (DMT)	45-minutes psychosis, businessman's special, DMT

The PO must also be familiar with work furlough programs. Work furlough enables a prisoner to work within the community. The parolee who experiences stable employment will generally be successful under supervision. Similarly, the PO needs to be aware of the multitude of agencies and organizations in the community that can be of assistance to his/her clients. The types of programs and agencies which may be of assistance include: child care programs, drug treatment programs, basic education programs, emergency assistance programs, financial assistance programs, food and clothing assistance centers, health programs, job placement programs, job training programs, and vocational rehabilitation programs. Finally, some city and state governments compile information on services available for offenders and should be consulted for assistance.

References

Administrative Office of the United States.(1981,January) Classification and supervision planning system. Washington, DC: Probation Division.

Administrative Office of the United States Courts. (1978). The presentence investigation report. Monograph No. 105. Washington, DC: Author.

Carney, L. P. (1977).Corrections and the community, Englewood Cliffs, NJ: Prentice-Hall.

Federal Judicial Center. An introduction to the federal probation system. Washington, DC: Author, FJC No. 76-1.

Friday, P. C. & Peterson, D. M. (1973). Shock imprisonment: Comparative analysis of short-term incarceration as a treatment technique. Canadian Journal of Criminology and Corrections,15:3,287-288.

Government of District of Columbia. (1973). Offender services in the Washington metropolitan area. Washington, DC: Author.

Serrill, M. (1974, September). From "bums" to businessmen: The Delancy Street Foundation. Corrections Magazine, 1, No. 1, 14.

Smith, M. A. (1973). As a matter of fact: An introduction to federal probation. Washington, DC: Federal Judicial Center.

State and county probation: System in crisis. A report to the Congress by the Comptroller General of the United States, May 27, 1976.

Thalmeimer, D. J. (1975) Cost analysis of correctional standards: Halfway houses. Vol. II. Washington, DC: U.S. Government Printing Office.

The society of alcoholics anonymous. (1949, November). American Journal of Psychiatry, 106, 5.

U.S. Department of Justice. (1971). Terms and symptoms of drug abuse. Washington, DC: Bureau of Narcotics and Dangerous Drugs.

Chapter 5

COUNSELING TECHNIQUES:
DEVELOPING AN EFFECTIVE STRATEGY

LEARNING OBJECTIVES

* To promote an understanding of the origins and principles of selected counseling techniques.

* To demonstrate the need for implementing counseling techniques in probation and parole operations.

* To explain the operational dynamics of applied counseling techniques.

DISCUSSION QUESTIONS

1. Briefly explain the central ideas underlying selected counseling theories.

2. Give examples of the successful application of counseling techniques by probation or parole officers, utilizing the counseling theories previously described.

3. What benefits may be gained from the successful mastery of these selected counseling approaches by probation and parole officers?

IMPORTANT TERMS

Reality therapy
Rational emotive therapy
Behavior modification
Transactional analysis
Group counseling

Career counseling
Psychodrama
Client centered approach
Crisis intervention
Art therapy

NAMES TO REMEMBER

William Glasser
Albert Ellis
B. F. Skinner

Jacob Moreno
Carl Rogers
Eric Berne

COUNSELING TECHNIQUES: DEVELOPING AN EFFECTIVE STRATEGY

Perhaps the most overlooked and often ignored responsibility of a probation or parole officer involves his or her counseling responsibilities. Yet, these duties probably comprise the most critical phase of probation and parole practice, if not in sheer time allotted, then at least in direct impact on client behavior. If client problems are to be resolved and the requirements of probation and parole met, counseling becomes the tool for accomplishing these tasks.

The following discussion will detail some of the origins, elements and applications of many of the more successful and pertinent counseling techniques in probation and parole practice. These approaches have sound theoretical foundations and have experienced wide acceptance and success in a variety of settings. Their application to probation and parole supervision appears logical, practical, and increasingly important. As the demands placed upon probation and parole functions continue to increase and the available resources to decline, innovations which increase effectiveness will become critical. Adding these ten basic counseling approaches to the existing repertoire of supervisory techniques can contribute to the profession's fulfillment of future societal expectations and criminal justice needs.

REALITY THERAPY

Reality therapy attempts to develop in a very short period of time those qualities which should have been established during the normal maturation process of an individual. It rejects the classical approach that views problems as the result of mental illness or severe behavior disorders. In place of such categorizations, the terms "responsible" and "irresponsible" are used and concentration is directed toward the present, not the unchangeable past. The primary goal of the reality therapist is to assist clients in learning better ways to fulfill their needs.

Proponent - William Glasser

William Glasser is a reknowned psychiatrist who has included in his vast clinical experiences work in juvenile institutions and hospital settings. Perhaps Glasser is best known for his popular book, Reality Therapy: A New Approach to Psychiatry (1975). Upon completing his psychiatric training, Glasser openly expressed doubts about some of the fundamental principles of conventional psychiatry which led him to search for new, practical approaches. This inquisitiveness and recognition of the need for new and viable methods of counseling resulted in the formulation of a theoretical approach called "reality" therapy.

Principles and Application

There are 14 principles of reality therapy which can be applied to probation or parole work. The following illustrations relate these principles in a probation setting.

Principle 1: Get involved: the effective PO needs to develop a warm, friendly, and personal relationship with the client. Involvement takes place between two people much like the same process that results in the development of friendship. Without involvement, longlasting behavioral and attitudinal changes rarely occur with clients.

Principle 2: The PO should reveal his or her own personality to the client in an effort to serve as a model for establishing openness in communication. Through this process, the client can follow the PO's example and express his or her fears and concerns.

Principle 3: The PO should encourage the client to use the personal pronouns "I" and "me" as much as possible in conversation. This process will insure that conversations between the PO and client are more meaningful. For example, if an unemployed client spends hours talking "about" the unemployment problem rather than personalizing his or her own job situation, time and energy is wasted.

Principle 4: In conversing with the client, the PO should talk in the "here and now." For instance, hours spent talking about early childhood difficulties will not necessarily help the client with his or her current unemployment situation.

Principle 5: The focus of a counseling session with a client should concern his or her actual daily behavior patterns. Spending lengthy periods of time in counseling sessions talking exclusively about feelings tends to not bring about desired behavioral changes.

Principle 6: A PO must ask "what" behavior a client exhibits, rather than "why" her or she exhibits such behavior. Asking a client "why" he or she did not find a job may result in needless excuses. The PO must try to determine what behavior the client is demonstrating that has prevented him or her from gaining employment and then work to change the undersired behavior. For example, the client may be unable to complete a job application form. The PO should assist the client, as much as possible, in gaining the skills needed to complete the job application.

Principle 7: The PO must request certain key questions of the client. First, what does the client think of his or her behavior? Second, is the behavior doing them any good? Behavior change is not likely to take place unless clients evaluate their behavior and its effects, and understand the important influences of their environment. Additionally, the clients must decide that their behavior is non-productive and they must desire to do something to improve it.

Principle 8: The PO, in his or her effort to assist a client, may ask, "What can be done about this problem?" The PO and client can then engage in a brainstorming session. This involves mobilizing one's creative capacities to work out a reasonable step-by-step resolution of the problem. The PO provides input and makes his or her own suggestions. Together, they seek to formulate a detailed and concrete plan which relies on common sense to remedy the identified problem. The PO and client may even role-play and rehearse the details of the plan to increase the chances for its successful completion.

Principle 9: The PO should ask the client additional questions once a plan has been perfected. First, will the client carry out this plan? Second, how can the PO know that the client will? Third, will the client give his or her promise? Fourth, will the client shake hands on it? Fifth, is the client willing to sign a contract? A client is more likely to live up to a plan if there is a commitment, a contract, or a formal agreement.

Principle 10: The PO should verify if the plan has been carried out. If the client has failed to carry out the plan, the PO should not waste time scolding or arguing with the client. The PO should not spend time listening to excuses provided by the person as to why the plan failed. The PO makes better use of the time with the client by asking: "Is the contract still in force, or is renegotiation needed?"

Principle 11: The PO does not give up on the client. He continues working with the client by maintaining concern, friendship, and involvement. The PO continues his or her efforts despite failures, broken promises and missed appointments.

Principle 12: The PO should praise as well as encourage the client to "keep up the good work." The smallest amount of success on the part of the client could be the beginning of a new way of life. Failure oriented people often do not believe others are genuinely interested in them as human beings.

Principle 13: The PO should be aware of the powerful and therapeutic impact of humor. Smiling, laughing, kidding, and joking are valuable tools for intensifying involvement and helping the client.

Principle 14: The PO should use group counseling as much as possible when working with clients. Through the use of groups, clients become aware of the successes of others, and can evaluate the plans used by others in overcoming crises.

Summary

Reality Therapy is directed toward achieving involvement in an open and honest human relationship. The clients may come to realize that someone is actually concerned about them and their progress, and that the PO will provide them with assistance. The critical elements of reality therapy may be summarized as follows: (1) the basic therapeutic job of the PO (reality therapist) is to become involved with the client; (2) when confronted with reality by the PO, the client is forced to decide whether he or she will opt for the responsible path; and (3) reality may be painful and even harsh to the client. It may also be difficult, as reality changes slowly. Persons should struggle to resolve their problems and enjoy the rewards that follow. A final point to remember is that the PO who utilizes reality therapy should not give up on a client. If the client fails at completing the plan, an additional opportunity to pursue an alternate course should be provided.

RATIONAL EMOTIVE PSYCHOTHERAPY

Rational emotive psychotherapy or rational emotive therapy (RET) is based on the assumption that irrational thinking is a major cause of problems for some individuals. These psychological problems arise from faulty perceptions (mistaken cognitions). Frequently, such problems result from severe emotional reactions to normal and unusual stimuli, and from habitually dysfunctional behavior patterns that may cause repetitive and non-adjustive responses (e.g., prolonged periods of depression resulting from stress of unemployment). Rational emotive therapy postulates that perceived emotional responses are caused by the unconscious evaluations and interpretations of events that are experienced. As a result, persons may feel anxious or depressed because they are convinced that failures are terrible, and rejections are painful. These individuals typically become very hostile when others are perceived to be acting unfairly toward them. The role of the therapist is to help the client alter such perceptions and respond to life situations more rationally.

Proponent - Albert Ellis

Albert Ellis, a leading clinical psychologist, has enjoyed a distinguished career both as an academician and practitioner. He authored hundreds of articles and the well-known book, A New Guide to Rational Living (1973). Ellis describes rational emotive psychotherapy as a comprehensive approach to psychological treatment that deals not only with the emotional and behavioral aspects of human disturbance, but places a great deal of emphasis on its "thinking" components (the human mind). Ellis believes that human beings are complex and do not generally become emotionally disturbed for the same reasons. Similarly, there is no single way to help persons who are disturbed.

Principles and Application

The PO using RET should begin the first session by identifying a few central irrational philosophies of life held by the client. The PO can suggest to the client how these ideas may lead to his or her emotional problems by demonstrating clinical symptoms, and by helping the client to question and challenge his or her irrational ideas. Often the PO induces the client to replace existing negative perceptions with improved feelings about the world, which may prevent future emotional difficulties.

The technique utilized in RET follows an A-B-C format. According to Ellis' view of emotions, point A is the situation (the activating event), point B is the belief system (attitudes, values and philosophies of an individual), point C is the consequences (one's feelings and behavior), point D is the disputation of the irrational beliefs, and finally, point E is the new emotional consequence. An example of the A-B-C theory of emotional disturbance in a probation or parole setting will assist in understanding its potential use. For instance, the activating event (point A) would occur when a girlfriend or boyfriend breaks the news to a client that he/she is going with another, and therefore wishes to break off the relationship. Point B involves the belief or interpretation of the event or fact, which might result in the client saying, "I really must be a worthless person," or, "I'll never find another great woman like her," or, "she doesn't want me, therefore, no one could possibly want me," or, "she shouldn't be that way, I can't stand the world being so unfair." Each illustrates a belief system that is not very rational. Point C involves the upsetting emotional consequence. In such a case, one feels depressed, or hostile, or both. The reaction is the product of the belief system. Point D consists of the PO disputing the irrational beliefs. Where is there evidence that the person who wishes to end a relationship is worthless? Is the breaking up proof that the client will never be able to have a satisfying relationship with anyone else, or that he or she will not be happy alone? In addition, why should one not expect the world to have injustices and fallible human beings? Point E represents the "new" emotional consequence. It relies on the assumption that one should be sad and annoyed rather than depressed and hostile. An expression of sadness for the probationer might be: "Well, we did have a nice relationship and I'm sorry to see it end, but it did have problems, and now I can go out and find someone else." Or an annoyed remark might be: "It is frustrating to find out that she was seeing someone, but it isn't the end of the world."

The view of the ABC approach is that probationers, and no one else, created their emotional feelings. No matter how inappropriately others behave, it is not the activating behavior but the probationer's "belief" about that behavior which proves upsetting. Everytime the probationer feels upset, depressed, or fearful and hostile, he or she may be reacting to both a rational and irrational belief. The rational belief may be: "I don't like this, it is unfortunate, and I wish I could change it." The irrational belief may take the following form:

"This is awful!   I can't stand it!   It shouldn't exist!
I'm a rotten person for allowing it to exist!"

If the probationer consistently and persistently
disputes, challenges, and questions his or her irrational
beliefs, those beliefs may eventually be minimized or
eliminated. If one continues this kind of disputing
behavior whenever one feels upset, a different more non-
demanding and productive philosophy of life can be
arrived at which may prevent constant frustrations.

The following is another example of the ABC approach
to emotions and how it might be used successfully.
Activating event A occurs when the client in a group
counseling session states, "I worked all night and the
pay is low. I've also got an unfair boss!" The
activating event results in B, the belief about the
event. The client in this case is likely to believe:
"It's too bad! Things should be better for me!" B leads
to C (a resulting emotion) in which the client feels
rotten, as shown by his or her response: "I'm depressed,
angry!" The next step is D which involves disputing and
challenging the attitudes and beliefs of the client by
the PO. The PO is likely to comment: "First, you don't
work all night. You work just part of the night." The
client answers, "That's correct." The PO then replies,
"And you say the pay is low, only $5.00 an hour. That is
substantially above minimum wage.   In addition, you know
you could be out of work." Disputing leads to step E, a
new emotional consequence.   The PO asks how the client
feels. The client remarks: "You know, maybe the job is
not all that bad."

Rational emotive therapy is a short-term process.
Probationers and parolees are educated with the ABC's and
given homework assignments. These assignments involve
risks, putting themselves in uncomfortable or anxiety-
producing situations, and learning to dispute irrational
beliefs about these situations. Homework assignments are
frequently given to the clients. For example, the client
who is frightened of subway trains is instructed to ride
several of them. In the next counseling session the PO
obtains the client's written thoughts about this
activity.

Rational emotive psychotherapy can also be used to
work with groups of clients who are having difficulties
with alcoholism. Alcoholics frequently consider
themselves as bad persons--unreliable, insincere, or
dishonest. Such persons may feel that everyone is
looking down on them. The alcoholic who believes that

everyone feels this way is engaging in irrational, nonproductive thinking. This thinking may seriously hamper his or her attempts to make a successful adjustment in the community.

Using RET in alcoholic groups enables the group members to confront and challenge each other about their irrational beliefs. For example, if one of the members of the alcoholic group states that he or she is angry because someone referred to him or her as a rotten person, the group may help this client examine this reaction. The group would help the client dispute such beliefs and aid in the formulation of a new emotional response. A group leader could also assist alcoholic members of the group in formulating individual homework assignments. The leader could then challenge, along with the other members of the group, the irrational beliefs expressed by different members of the group.

These techniques have been utilized in numerous settings. For instance, a federal probation office in Dallas, Texas established a group counseling program to assist probationers and parolees with their problems on an experimental basis. The director of the program used the ABC model to work with clients in group counseling sessions. It proved very successful (Ruhnow, 1975).

RET assumes that the essential basis for improvement or change in the individual is not the removal of his or her present symptoms, but rather a significant, deep-seated and lasting change in one's basic philosophy of life. RET stresses that certain core irrational ideas are at the root of most emotional disturbances. Ellis describes the following twelve common irrational ideas:

1. It is irrational to believe that is a dire necessity to be loved for everything one does;

2. It is irrational to consider people as bad, wicked, and in need of punishment;

3. It is irrational to consider past experiences and events as total determinants;

4. It is an irrational idea that one must be a perfectionist in order to be considered important;

5. It is irrational to feel that unwanted events are necessarily catastrophic;

6. It is irrational to feel that unhappiness is caused by outside circumstances over which the probationer has no control;

7. It is irrational to allow minor things to become major and continued worries;

8. It is irrational to assume that it is easier to avoid certain difficulties and self responsibilities than to face them;

9. It is irrational to be extremely upset over other people's problems and disturbances;

10. It is irrational to believe that one should be overly dependent on others;

11. It is irrational to believe that there is always a right or perfect solution to every problem and it must be found or the results will be terrible; and

12. It is irrational to dictate that the world, and especially other people, must be totally fair and just to make life worthwhile.

Summary

RET demonstrates that no matter what the client's basic irrational philosophy of life is, or how he or she acquired it, the person is presently disturbed because he or she believes the world is self-defeating. In RET, the client comes to recognize his or her thoughts. This individual will challenge and question these beliefs and will usually improve significantly. PO's should recognize that RET is a comprehensive counseling technique that particularly lends itself to application in the probation and parole setting. Its complexity can be overcome through a proper understanding of its critical elements and the effective use of its simply stated principles. As stated by Epictetus in the first century A.D.: "Men are disturbed not by things, but the views they take of them" (Patterson, 1973, p. 51).

GROUP COUNSELING

Group counseling in a probation and parole setting provides the client with the tools for exploring and understanding oneself by examining personal values and norms of behavior. It requires a client to express his or her problems in a group setting where participants can react to the client's concerns.

Proponent - George M. Gazda

Group counseling has become widely accepted and applied in diverse settings to the extent that no single proponent should be given primary credit for the development and success it has experienced. The research on group counseling has grown rapidly with increasingly positive results. George M. Gazda, author of Group Counseling: A Development Approach (1971), has become known as a leading developer of group counseling, providing ideas and techniques for conducting group counseling that can have immediate benefits for probation and parole professionals.

Principles and Application

A group provides an economical use of a PO's time. While a PO may be able to work with 15 clients in a group in an hour's time, he or she can only see two or three clients in the same period of time on a one-to-one basis.

The group counseling process facilitates an effective use of peer group pressure. As an illustration: If there are 13 clients in the group, one of whom is talking about drinking difficulties and the other clients are questioning the client about his or her drinking habits, this peer interaction will probably have a greater effect on changing the client's view toward drinking than a PO's advice.

Another advantage of group counseling concerns training new PO's as group leaders. For example, new Federal Probation Officers in the United States Court for the District of Columbia are given the opportunity to act as observers in group counseling sessions. By observing the group process they gain insight into processes for conducting their own groups in the future.

One type of group counseling that can take place in a probation or parole office setting involves employment groups. Probationers or parolees selected for this type of group are those who are having problems in securing and maintaining steady employment. The group may focus on employment questions such as: What type of job am I best equipped for? How do I approach someone for a job? Where do I seek this type of work? If I do get a job, how do I get along with my fellow employees?

How may my employer help me once I get the job? The goals of this group are to aid and assist probationers and parolees having problems in the employment area to bring their problems into the open and express them in a group setting. Furthermore, it is possible to have role playing activities to teach clients how to obtain jobs and how to succeed in employer-employee relationships.

A PO who runs a group counseling session has a great deal of impact on the success or failure of the group. He or she must be sure each client in the group has an opportunity to be heard. In addition, the PO must frequently focus the attention of the group on what is happening within the group. For example, he or she might say, "Were you aware that only two persons in this group voiced an opinion?" This type of comment should facilitate further discussion. Giving simple directions is also the responsibility of the PO in a group setting. For example, he or she may structure the group by having the clients complete name tags or suggest some exercise in which the group should participate. Sullivan (1952) advised that the group atmosphere should be as friendly, informal, and democratic as possible.

The group leader may have to intervene to keep group members from overexposure. Overexposure involves sharing personal feelings that may not facilitate the group or the group goals, or feelings which create a situation where neither the clients nor the group leader are capable of properly functioning. The PO as group leader may decide to protect a group member, if he or she feels remarks from the group are ill-timed or unnecessarily severe. A group leader may at times help a client maintain his or her identity despite group pressures to change the person's views.

It is often advantageous to have two PO's act as group co-leaders. Jones and Pheiffer (1975) have long advocated the use of co-leaders in a group. One leader can work with clients experiencing significant emotional problems while the other leader assists remaining group members in dealing with their reactions to the situation. By working as a team, the two officers are able to monitor and facilitate individual and group development better than either could alone.

There are many roles that may be played by group leaders and clients. For example, an "information seeker" assumes the role of trying to clarify problems being discussed in the group. The "information giver," on the other hand, relates his or her own experience to the group problem. The "encourager" praises, agrees with, and accepts the contributions of others in the group.

The PO counseling a group generally finds it helpful to establish ground rules. One ground rule might be that each group member tries to be as honest as possible in the expression of his or her views. Another ground rule may promote realism. Experience has shown that if group members know the group will be candid and reality-oriented, they do not pretend.

The PO should realize that no two members of a group will derive the same benefit from the group experience. The value of the group to the client will depend in large measure upon the degree of prevailing acceptance, the quality of the interaction, client self-perception and interest in other group members, and the group process utilized.

Some PO's have found that it is effective to label groups according to their goals. For example, an employment group would have the goals of achieving employment for each group member. A family group on the other hand would have as its primary goal the discussion of problems facing clients and their families.

An additional important consideration, relates to the incentive of the client in participating in the counseling process. This means that a probationer who fails to take part in the probation office group counseling program is subject to a possible revocation of probation.

The ultimate goal of any group counseling session in a probation or parole setting is to increase a client's chances of succeeding. Kelman (1963) lists the following goals which he considers to be benefits achieved by the group process:

1. to help an individual overcome feelings of isolation;

2. to enhance self-esteem and increase acceptance of self;

3. the group should help develop hope for improved adjustment;

4. to help each individual learn to be himself and to express his real feelings;

5. a group should help an individual accept responsibility for himself and for solving his problems;

6. a group process should help an individual develop, practice and maintain new relationship skills;

7. a group should help an individual enhance his commitment to change his attitude and behavior;

8. a group should enable an individual to operationalize his insights and skills by applying them in his daily life.

Summary

Group counseling seeks human learning and problem-solving through social interaction. It improves the social learning process by highlighting the dynamics of the group and not environmental factors. Group members, guided by a leader, are encouraged to share individual and interpersonal feelings and perceptions. The atmosphere proves conducive to both independence and interdependence, and stresses the healthy attributes of each. A frequent benefit from group counseling is the assumption of responsibility by the clients and a knowledge of the assistance and support available from their peers in overcoming problems. It also promotes a forum for discovering desirable alternatives for apparently unsolvable dilemmas. Overall, group counseling provides both an environment and a process in which numerous counseling goals can be met (Kratcoski, 1981).

CAREER COUNSELING

Finding a job is not an easy task, particularly during periods of high unemployment and changing economies. It is especially difficult for a probationer or parolee. Since the PO is charged with the responsibility of assisting the unemployed client in finding a job, career counseling becomes an important task.

Proponent - Eli Ginzberg

Eli Ginzberg (1972) is one among many students and proponents of career counseling. Ginzberg's research confirmed that a job choice is a lifelong process. In this process, the individual typically seeks a job which fits his or her career preparation and goals, as well as the realities of the work world. Especially pertinent in recent years, these realities are frequently changing, and result in constant reappraisals of job options and continuing needs for career counseling.

Principles and Application

How does the PO discover the employment potential and career goals of the client? The answer basically lies in the interviewing process and the presentence investigation report (PSI). The PSI will usually contain information on the client's work history over recent years. It will report the individual's earnings, whether the person was promoted or fired, and reasons for any change in jobs. By reading the PSI, the PO will formulate realistic ideas regarding job possibilities for the client.

The "interview" also provides the PO with the opportunity to ask pertinent questions about the client's work background. This interview typically takes place in the office. For example, does the client still have an interest in the welding trade? The PSI may indicate that the person worked as a welder for ten years prior to arrest and conviction, leading the PO to try to discover whether the interest in that occupation continues. If this client desires a career change, what options are available? A testing of the client's interests and abilities may be required. The Kuder General Interest Survey (KGIS), the Strong Vocational Interest Blank (1974) and the Ohio Vocational Interest Survey (1970) are tests that may reveal vocational interest areas of the client. The KGIS has numerous interest scales which include: outdoor, mechanical, computational, scientific, persuasive, artistic, literary, musical, social service, and clerical areas (Kuder, 1965).

Federal and state publications also assist the PO in identifying specific qualities required of particular jobs. One publication, Dictionary of Occupational Titles (1965), provides an index of industries and jobs. For instance, if the client wants to be a truck driver, what requirements are demanded? Does the applicant need a diploma from a truck driving school? Such career advice can provide valuable information in assisting the client in a job search.

Once the client has identified a job that appears interesting and has attainable application requirements, the next step may involve education and training. If there are indications that a high school diploma (or GED) is required for the particular job, the client without a high school diploma should consider enrolling in an adult education program.

After the client has completed the required education or training he or she then begins the difficult task of exploring job opportunities. Newspaper ads, state employment office job listings, and industry job announcements are several sources of information which identify available jobs.

The PO can also offer substantial assistance in preparing the client for the actual job interview. Through the use of role-playing, the client can learn the art of successful expression for job interviews. The client must learn that punctuality as well as neat appearance is very important in any job interview.

Once the client gains employment, the role of the PO as job counselor does not end. He or she must reinforce positive work progress made by the client and confront the client when he or she fails at job tasks. The PO who assist clients in their quest for employment will find that employed clients are generally more successful in fulfilling the conditions of probation or parole.

Summary

Career counseling is a tremendous responsibility of the PO and can be performed with relative ease if undertaken with care and determination—although some variables (e.g., economy and employment opportunities) remain beyond the officer's control. The primary tasks of the office becomes one of advisement, and identifying and reinforcing the desires and abilities of the job seeker to the existing job market. By developing and applying the proven techniques of successful career counseling, this job becomes both attainable and personally rewarding.

PSYCHODRAMA

Psychodrama attempts to provide an accurate portrayal of a client's present, past, and future actions through a variety of techniques. The client's self-expression and freedom of communication leads to improved self-understanding and personality reorientation.

Psychodrama requires the reenactment of life situations in which the individual's relationships (real or imagined) are acted out in the form of a role which he or she chooses to portray. Other actors may portray persons with whom the client is experiencing difficulty.

Proponent - Jacob L. Moreno

Jacob Moreno, a researcher with numerous talents and interests, began developing the counseling theory of psychodrama after his arrival in the United States in 1925. Moreno's endeavors included the following: dramatist, theologian, poet, philosopher, inventor, psychiatrist, sociodramatist, sociometrist and educator. With such an array of talents and skills, it was not surprising that he became the leading scholar on the concepts of psychodrama. Moreno wrote profusely on the topic and dedicated himself to the training of practitioners.

Principles and Application

Psychodrama normally requires clients to enact important phases of their lives in a group setting. A client may also play the role of an absent person in conflict reenactments. The group (or audience) participants may also serve as a sounding board for expressions of difficulty. They provide the client with corrective and reality oriented advice. Their reactions and advice should contain plausible solutions to problems. Furthermore, clients in the group can identify and share in the displayed feelings and emotions.

One technique used in psychodrama is that of role playing. This process helps clients to intensely express their feelings. In addition, clients can express feelings which they perceive others have toward them. Role playing is an effective procedure with unemployed clients. The PO can role play as a prospective employer. The unemployed client then undergoes the "employment" interview. By practicing the job interview, the unemployed client increases his or her chances of being successful during the actual process. Some PO's video

104

tape the practice job interview. This video tape session
is then shown to the unemployed client. This enables the
client to observe how he or she performed during the job
interview.

Roles   in psychodrama vary depending upon   the
client's age, sex, social situation, and personality
make-up.   Also, the nature of one's peers, siblings, and
marital relationships impact the formation of roles. The
PO   may   enact   the   behavior   of a   person   with
whom the client is having problems.   As the client sees
how his or her actions appear to others, a new insight of
desired behavior is gained. The PO, for example, can act
as   a   father, boss, teacher, police office or other
authority figure who causes difficulty for the client.
Thus, the client can discover new relationships based on
a   better   understanding of his or her interactions   with
role play figures.

Another   psychodrama   process   is   called   mirror
technique.   In this procedure another client plays the
role of the client who is experiencing problems but has
difficulty expressing them. The client who is having the
problem observes from the outside. Using this technique,
he can see him/herself, as if in a mirror.

Future   projection is a psychodrama technique which
helps the client to realize the anxiety he has of the
future. In the psychodramatic presentation of the future,
the client is required to portray two areas. First, he
must portray his wishes and desires; which may be
entirely unrealistic.   Second, he must portray   the
realistic perceptions of his future. It is important for
the client to portray what he or she feels will actually
take   place   in   the   future.   The client should be
encouraged to portray as completely as possible the
places, the persons, and the events of the future. The
more clearly future events are envisioned, the better the
client's chances will be to confront them.   In such
psychodramatic sessions, the client performs as his or
her own "prophet." The client is not only tested for the
future, but is prepared for it.

Summary

Psychodrama   enables the client to act out problems
(Nikelly, 1971).   Consequently, he or she can deal more
effectively with interpersonal situations. Through role
playing the client reveals his or her current life style.
Then, after constructive reorientation, the client is
able to originate alternative solutions to   present

situations. Clients are able to convey feelings and
information that otherwise would have been difficult to
communicate (Ohlsen, 1970). From this information, the
clients are able to understand the sources of their
difficulties, and thereby devise strategies for
effectively dealing with them. The simplicity with which
roles may be enacted allows this technique to be
successfully applied to a wide range of individuals.

CLIENT CENTERED THERAPY

"Client centered" therapy is based on the assumption
that an individual has the capacity to solve his or her
own problems (Shertzer, 1971). It is referred to by many
as a "person centered" approach in counseling. It has
been shown effective in a variety of settings, including
the following: education, marriage, leadership,
organizational development, conflict resolution, and the
facilitation of large group processes (International
Encyclopedia of the Social Sciences, 1979).

Proponent - Carl R. Rogers

Dr. Carl Rogers is considered to be the founder of
client centered psychotherapy. In 1951 he authored
Client Centered Therapy: Its Current Practice, Implica-
tions, and Theory. Since his original work, Rogers has
generalized and extended his research to new settings,
including school systems and the probation and parole
professions.

Principles and Application

The basic philosophy of the client centered PO is
represented by the counselor's attitude of respect for
the client and the right of the client to self-direction.
The nature of probation and parole work makes it
essential that the PO and client have a relatively close
relationship. The client centered approach should assist
the client in experiencing a feeling of safety. The
client will find that his or her attitudes are understood
by the PO, and not summarily rejected as being without
merit. The client is then able to explore and evaluate
his or her feelings and to gradually recognize possible
remedies. In a safe and secure counseling relationship
the client can perceive for the first time the hostile
meaning and purpose of certain types of behavior. In
addition, the client can understand why he or she has
felt guilty about the behavior and why it has been
necessary to deny the basis for the behavior.

The client with these new perceptions should find that the PO also shares similar perceptions, but with an accepting attitude. Generally, this acceptance is embraced by the client as well. The client, in essence, views his or her experiences more in terms of their effect on his or her personal development. Once the client has gained new insight and confidence, he or she can develop strategies to deal with particular problem situations.

In order for the PO to be effective as a client centered counselor, he or she must have numerous qualities. The first quality is that of "acceptance." The PO should be accepting of the client as an individual. The PO accepts the person with his/her faults, including personality and behavior problems. Such an attitude is more than mutual acceptance, it is positive respect for the client as a person of worth.

The second trait of a client centered counselor is that of "congruence" (Ohlsen, 1970). This term implies that the PO is a real person who lacks phony or superficial qualities. The PO is not just playing a role but is consistent in his/her actions and advice.

The third characteristic which is desirable for the PO using the client centered approach is that of "under-standing." The PO tries to sense the client's private world as if it were his or her own. Such understanding enables the client to explore feelings freely and deeply, and with greater comprehension. This understanding does not simply involve traditional diagnosis or evaluation, which are external in nature. The desire of the PO "to understand" is more readily accepted by the client, and is generally conducive to progress.

The fourth trait a client centered counselor should possess is the ability to "communicate" the qualities of acceptance, congruence, and understanding. It is of no value for the PO to be accepting, congruent, and understanding, if the client does not perceive it. Therefore, it is very important that acceptance, congruence, and understanding be effectively communicated to the client. The PO who has these attitudes or characteristics should express them as naturally and spontaneously as possible. The choice of words used by the PO is important, because it sets the tone of the counseling relationship with the client (Cuttle, 1980). Both verbal and non-verbal communication should be employed by the PO. The PO may wish to embrace as well as commend the client for his or her success. The

effective use of this approach may insure that a
favorable relationship develops (Rogers, 1951). This
relationship is perceived by the client as safe, secure,
free from threats, and supporting. Likewise, the PO is
perceived as dependable, trustworthy, and consistent.
The resulting relationship between the PO and client is
one in which positive change can occur. Clients
experience new feelings of openness which lead to a
deeper understanding of themselves and restore the path
to self-improvement.

Yalom (1975) states that in the ideal counselor-
client relationship, the following results should take
place when the client centered therapy approach is
correctly used:

1. The client is increasingly free in expressing
    his or her feelings.

2. The client begins to test reality. He or she
    develops discriminatory feelings and perceptions
    of the environment, other persons, and new
    experiences.

3. The client increasingly becomes aware of the
    incongruity between his or her experiences and
    self concept.

4. The client becomes aware of feelings which have
    been previously denied or distorted.

5. The client's self concept becomes more realistic
    and genuine because of his or her counseling
    experience.

6. The client becomes increasingly able to
    experience, without threat, the PO's
    unconditional, positive attitude toward him.

7. The client increasingly evaluates his or her
    behavior.

8. The client reacts less to evaluations by
    others and more to the effect of events on his
    or her own development.

Summary

Client centered therapy hypothesizes that
individuals have within themselves the necessary
intrinsic forces for orderly growth, which may at times

be hindered. Related to this central organizing tendency is a drive for achieving self-actualization. By developing the proper conditions and using the appropriate techniques, the desired actualizing forces may be released. As a result, the PO may assist the client in freeing these important capacities.

CRISIS INTERVENTION

Crisis and probation/parole work may often seem synonymous. Crisis intervention techniques enable the PO to deal with critical problems and crises that may arise doing field investigations. Most early works in this field dealt with crisis in family situations, but the principles may be more broadly applied (Harper, 1975).

Proponents - Jeffrey A. Schwartz and David A. Liebman

Schwartz and Liebman (1975) developed a crisis intervention training course for criminal justice personnel which provides the average probation officer with those skills necessary for dealing effectively with dispute situations which he or she encounters in day to day activities. Problems addressed by this crisis intervention training model are diverse: general street violence; black and white fights; disputes between parents and a probationer; arguments caused by alcohol or drugs; and other problems that arise among people in domestic situations or field investigations.

Principles and Application

Approaching the location of a field investigation or conducting a home visit can be dangerous for a PO (Erickson, 1972). The PO should check the streets around the location of his or her visit for problems (e.g., loiterers or juvenile gangs). If the PO notices suspicious groups "hanging out", he or she should attempt to avoid them or postpone the visit until the problem conditions improve.

Crisis intervention includes the application of measures to avoid creating or enlarging crisis situations. Defusing techniques assist a PO in restoring order in potentially violent situations. The "request" approach is often effective. For example, a person who is hysterically crying is likely to respond to trivial requests, which may channel concentration away from the emotional ordeal being experienced. In the process the client is more likely to become less emotional and start to communicate in a calm manner. The "Columbo approach" is another defusing technique. For example, although the PO can clearly see what the client is arguing about, he or she can pretend to be unaware of the conflict which is taking place, forcing the participants to explain the crisis rather than continue it.

Another element in crisis intervention is "mediation," which may include the process of resolving a client's family feud. The PO tempts to work out something constructive with the disputants, rather than making an arrest or some more drastic measure. The goal of mediation is to help the client and his or her family agree to a specific course of action and to leave them with a positive feeling about their decision. The final agreement reached may be the idea of one of the disputants, but more frequently it will be a compromise which represents the interests of both parties.

There are certain things a PO should avoid when mediating a domestic quarrel. He or she should avoid warning or threatening statements. For example, "Mr. and Mrs. Smith, if you continue to fight, I will have your child taken away from you." Another behavior to avoid is judging or criticizing. For example, "Mr. Smith, you're being pretty disgusting right now." Such comments will likely raise the level of tension and provide an additional obstacle to resolving the dispute.

An important feature of crisis intervention is "referral." Referral is the process of getting a commitment from the disputants that they will seek a community resource for help in managing specific problems. An example would be the client who is experiencing a drinking problem. In this instance a referral might be made to an Alcoholics Anonymous (AA) group for the client and his or her relatives.

A crisis may be encountered by a citizen at several points in the criminal justice process. Situations of particular concern are: (1) the arrest and initial detention stage; (2) the presentence phase (3) the revocation of probation phase; and (4) upon release from an institution and return to the community. The attitude and verbal as well as non-verbal communication of the PO can greatly increase or decrease the anxiety level of the client during these periods. With most defendants, discussions with the PO can be positive. Defendants can be motivated by the PO to use their time to find jobs, enroll in training or treatment programs, or begin working on inter-personal relationship problems.

110

The new parolee is a prime candidate for the application of crisis intervention theory. He or she may face crisis problems of unemployment, lack of housing, or new family responsibilities. With such problems it is important for a PO to keep in mind the crisis concept of breaking down the total problem into smaller, more manageable parts. The unemployed parolee, for example, may need to first learn the proper method of completing a job application, before actually applying and interviewing for a job. Hence, crisis intervention may be considered to include crisis prevention.

Summary

Crisis intervention principles enable a PO to handle problems in a more sensible and controlled manner. They also increase the chances for clients to become productive members of society. The PO must be aware that while not every client is in a state of crisis, many may face potential crisis situations. Although clients may not desire or be responsive to crisis intervention techniques, they still may be needed. Crisis intervention theory can certainly be an important source of knowledge to use if and when the need arises in the course of one's job as a probation or parole officer.

ART THERAPY

Art therapy with clients is a recent development available to modern probation and parole. Art therapy may be defined as the process of using art for the client to communicate his or her thoughts, feelings, and anxieties to others.

Proponent - Margaret Naumberg

Art therapy, like group counseling, has experienced a gradual and progressive development in the United States. One of the primary developers of modern art therapy concepts has been Margaret Naumberg, a New York psychologist and author of numerous texts on art therapy techniques. One of her most widely acclaimed books, An Introduction to Art Therapy (1973), has served as a guide for practitioners in diagnosing and treating behavior problems in children. These same techniques have been refined and applied in the adult setting with similar success. The basic techniques of art therapy involve the client producing a series of drawings and then rendering interpretations of them. The therapist generally asks questions, offers interpretations, and encourages more drawing. This process gradually results in a more trusting relationship between the therapist and client, and opens a line of communication conducive to a productive interchange of thoughts and ideas. Within such an atmosphere, probation and parole duties may be performed with increased ease and effectiveness.

Principles and Application

How does a PO use art therapy in an office setting? The answer lies in the "Before, Now, and After" art therapy technique. This process can be used with an individual client or group of clients.

The application of art therapy is not difficult and can be performed in a straightforward fashion. For example, the client is given three pieces of blank poster paper and a drawing marker. He/she is instructed by the PO to write the word "Before" on the top of the first poster, "Now" on the second poster, and "After" on the third. The PO then instructs the client or clients (if in a group setting), to think about the words "Before," "Now" and "After" in terms of their probation or parole status. In other words, what was their life like before they received a criminal sentence? Secondly, what is their life like now? Thirdly, what do they see in the future for themselves after their conditions are completed? They are told to draw what their life was like before, what it is like now, and what they see for themselves in the future. They are typically given 30 to 45 minutes to complete this task. Once the clients have completed the task of "drawing their lives" they are asked to present their "drawings" to the group. Each client must explain the meaning of his or her drawings to the group. For example, the client with all "Before" pictures of money and needles explains that before receiving probation he spent his money on the purchase of his heroin habit. This art therapy technique has been used with new probationers/parolees in group counseling sessions at the U.S. Probation Office in Washington, D.C. where it proved beneficial. The "Before, Now, After" art technique forced clients to reflect on their lives and to provide the PO with indicators of their thoughts.

An example of a common "Before" drawing is the picture of a stick figure surrounded by other stick figures. The interpretation of such a picture may reveal that before probation the client had many friends. The second picture in such a series might be a stick figure standing alone. The interpretation would be that the probationer has lost his or her friends while on probation. A third picture would generally be a picture of a stick figure surrounded by other stick figures. The interpretation would be that the probationer anticipates the finding of new friends after the probation period has ended.

Using the art therapy technique of "Before, Now, and After," clients learn that their problems are not unique. They learn that other clients have faced similar problems and have common hopes for the future. This technique has many advantages for the PO. The PO learns of the common problems faced by clients. It may be discovered that a problem of a new client is one of unemployment. As a result, an "employment" counseling group can be created so that unemployed clients can regularly meet to make plans in combating their common problems. The PO, in time, is likely to have increased communications with the clients.

Various researchers have successfully utilized art therapy in their research. Dr. Hanscarl Leuner (1969) concludes that art therapy enables an individual to express his or her emotions with less anxiety. By reducing the anxiety the individual improves his or her ability to communicate. Art therapist Reyher (1963) found that art therapy gives a client a unique opportunity to explore topics meaningful to his or her future behavior. Similarly, another leading therapist, Landgarten (1981), discovered that the process of art therapy enables one to explore in greater depth an individual's strengths as well as faults. Further research is bound to reveal even more benefits.

Summary

Art therapy, like many additional counseling approaches, can be important in discovering the true feelings and fears of clients. While many clients may be unable or hesitant to verbally express their feelings to a supervisory official, these same individuals may be able to communicate their thoughts through art therapy. This process can improve the supervisor/client relationship by opening up the channels of communication in a relatively unobstrusive manner. The information gained from this therapy can be used in numerous ways, including: the improvement of one's self-concept; the remedying of present obstacles to reform; and the selection of realistic future goals which will serve present probation or parole needs.

TRANSACTIONAL ANALYSIS

Transactional analysis (TA) enables a PO to assist a client through effective communication. TA assumes that a client generally communicates on one of three basic levels: adult, parent, or child. These three levels provide working indicators of the client's mental processes and behavior. By understanding the communication process more precisely, the PO is better able to undertake the counseling that is needed, and to gather the information necessary for supervision.

Proponent - Eric Berne

Eric Berne is considered by many to be the father of transactional analysis. He established the conceptual framework for his communication model in his bestseller, Games People Play (1964).

Althought the work of Berne was embraced and expanded by others, the most significant contributions to his model were perhaps made by Thomas Harris in his book, I'm OK - You're OK (1967). Harris soon gained recognition as a pioneer in the application of transactional analysis to the treatment of psychiatric patients. In the field of criminal justice two articles relating transactional analysis to the problems of probation and parole officers have appeared in Federal Probation (Nicholson, 1970; Frazier, 1972).

While transactional analysis has been widely read and accepted as an important technique for defining and analyzing communication interactions in the business community (Robbins, 1980), investigation of its applications to the criminal justice system's operations have been limited. Although certain aspects of transactional analysis are being used intuitively, it would seem important for probation and parole professionals to better understand and more effectively implement this technique in their supervision and management practices.

Principles and Application

While the intricacies of TA theory can be examined in great detail and its several components woven into a pattern of complex relationships, the basic elements can be explained in a straightforward fashion and their benefits easily recognized. According to Berne and Harris, one's personality and behavior can be categorized into one of the following ego states: parent, adult, and

child. Each of these ego states reflects modes of
behavior and communication patterns typical of the
parent, adult, or child stages of growth and development.
In simple terms, the parent within a person reflects
feelings and behavior similar to those demonstrated by
one's mother and father. A parent can be critical, or
helping, or both. The adult in a person serves to
examine facts objectively and to seek reasonable and
calculated solutions. An appropriate analogy to this ego
state is the information processing and decision making
capability of a computer. The child in a person operates
in a manner much like that of an actual child. The
feelings and behavior appear impulsive and reflect
immaturity and child-like reasoning.

Each of these three egos states can be used to
describe communications which frequently occur in the
probation or parole setting. For example, a PO acts in
the parent model when he/she lectures a client on
arriving late for their scheduled appointment. A PO may
act in the adult mode when he/she reasons with a client
on the best occupational alternatives for his or her
newly acquired job skills. Finally, clients may fit into
the child mode when they become convinced that society is
"out to get them." These three ego states provide
essential elements in analyzing levels or modes of
communication which can occur between two or more
individuals.

The dynamics of transactional analysis involve more
than merely categorizing ego states. TA also involves
the identification of repetitive sets of social maneuvers
(Starling, 1980). These maneuvers are commonly referred
to as pastimes, games, and scripts.

Pastimes involve interactions which occur in almost
ritualistic ways. For instance, a client and PO
frequently engage in an exchange of pleasantries upon
first meeting in order to "break the ice" or as a prelude
to establishing a working rapport. The interactions are
typically comfortable to the participants, but yield
little factual or specific information.

Games refer to a sequence of transactions which
occur with a definite pattern. Of special importance to
the game situation is the realization that such a
transaction has significance at two different levels--it
has both a surface and a hidden meaning. More clearly
stated, games are a series of human moves with a
"gimmick." Games have two chief characteristics: (1)
their ulterior quality, and (2) the payoff. While games

are certainly frequently played among probationers and parolees, they are not unique to these clients and can also be exhibited by probation and parole officers. For example, a PO may simultaneously attempt to help a client while making fun of the person. Thus, the officer's child state enjoys the game while his adult state considers the exercise productive.

Scripts, according to TA theory, are composed of even larger, more complex sets of transactions which are reflected in a person's behavior and feelings. Everyone is considered to have a "life script" or life plan, which evolves during his or her early formative years--whether the person is aware of it or not. The script can be either healthy or unhealthy. For example, some clients may have decided early in life that they should not trust or confide in others, since others will undoubtedly utilize the information against them (the clients). Such life scripts of distrust and self-reliance can have enormous repercussions in trying to effectively counsel clients in coping within a cooperative setting.

An integral part of games and scripts is the concept of "stroking." A stroke refers to a payoff and can be either verbal or nonverbal, and positive (producing good feelings) or negative (producing bad feelings). People are inclined to seek strokes to which they are accustomed, or which dominated their early personal development. Recognizing and learning to cope with the "stroking" needs of probationers and parolees is of special concern to PO's in counseling settings where they must be properly applied.

Finally, in analyzing communication transactions, the existence and importance of complementary, crossed, and ulterior transactions must be understood. Examples of each type of transaction will assist in an understanding of each.

A transaction is considered complementary when the initiator of the transaction receives a response from the target ego state in the other person. In other words, if a parole officer speaks from a parent state to the parolee in a child state and the parolee responds as anticipated (as a child to a parent), then the transaction is predicted, and some information is gained.

A crossed transaction occurs when the stimulus fails to get the anticipated response. Crossed transactions usually precipitate interpersonal conflicts and result in a breakdown of communication, although they also have potential for being used productively by alert and knowledgeable participants. A typical crossed transaction is exemplified by a PO (speaking from a parent state) who admonishes a client to "go to work," but the client (speaking from an adult state) inquires as to the availability of gainful employment for a person with his or her skill (or lack of skills) and a criminal record. In this instance, the unexpected or crossed response might serve to promote a more beneficial dialogue.

An ulterior transaction is more complex in nature and involves the activity of two ego states simultaneously--thus frequently providing a basis for games. A transaction which appears to be occurring on the adult-to-adult level may, in fact, reflect a psychological transaction taking place on a different level. For instance, a PO may comment to a client that he or she (the client) may eventually be incarcerated due to a lack of initiative in finding employment. The client may respond from an apparently adult perspective, while secretly harboring child state feelings of resentment which will ultimately determine his or her course of action.

The building blocks of TA theory are not necessarily complex and can provide valuable tools for describing, analyzing, and controlling transactions between criminal justice professionals and their clients. In the probation and parole setting, the techniques are especially useful and relatively easy to command. By further examining these transactions in relation to probation and parole practices, an improved understanding of their nature should evolve which can result in greater competency and higher levels of performance.

The following examples of transactions which can occur in the probation and parole setting are briefly analyzed below. While these exact scenarios may not be typical of the experiences found in any given organization, they are presented to illustrate the types and nature of transactions to which a probation or parole officer may well be acquainted.

Complementary transactions are characterized by an absence of conflict. The sender receives the intended type of response and the lines of communication are parallel. A complementary parent to parent exchange, for example, would be one where a PO (in the parent state) says to another PO (in the parent state); "Frank, that

Joe Powers ought to know better than that!" Frank
responds, "You are absolutely right." This might reflect
preexisting negative feelings toward Joe by the two
officers. An example of a complementary adult to adult
exchange is evidenced by the following exchange between a
PO and a secretary. Frank says, "Sally, do you have the
file?" Sally responds, "Yes, here it is." This is a
complementary adult to adult transaction, as a concise
and valuable exchange of information occurs.

Another complementary transaction would be a child
to child exchange of feelings. For example: Mark (in
his child state) says, "I cannot believe how stupid the
probation officers are around here!" Frank responds,
"Yeah, I am really fed up with them, and this whole lousy
place!" In this case, the exchange of feelings concerns
a topic they are both interested in, but little in the
way of productive information is procured.

Crossed-transactions can also be important to the
parole and probation function. A crossed-transaction is
a transaction in which the stimulus fails to get the
anticipated response. Crossed-transactions usually
precipitate interpersonal conflicts and can result in a
breakdown of communication. An example of crossed-
transaction may be a PO talking to his client. The PO
(speaking from an adult state) states uncritically,
"You look tired." The client might be expected to reply
in an adult fashion: "No, I'm really not" or "Yes, I
am." Instead, he responds from a child state, "Why are
you always criticizing me?" The transaction is crossed
and the PO's attempt at a productive dialogue is
jeopardized. A similar result may occur from the
following crossed-transaction: the PO says, "Don't talk
to me like that!" This is a parent to child transaction.
The client responds, "You shouldn't yell at me either."
This is parent to child response, and the potential for
communication problems emerge.

Ulterior transactions have hidden messages in them.
In an ulterior transaction, two messages are sent. One
is the obvious message. The other message is a secret
message that carries the real meaning in a transaction--
sometimes intentionally and sometimes not. Ulterior
messages often lead to bad feelings. The PO,for example,
says, "Since you have never held a job very long, why
don't you seek temporary employment?" The conversation
appears to be on an adult to adult level. However, on a
psychological level, the meaning is parent to child. The
true desire is to entice the client into obtaining full-
time employment.

According to transactional analysis theory everyone occasionally needs "strokes." A stroke may be as simple as a pat on the back or a word of recognition. If the PO greets a new client with a smile and handshake, it can constitute a stroke. Similarly, a PO who states to his client, "I'm proud that you went out and applied for the job I told you about," is giving the client a positive stroke because the client did something desired by the officer.

Here are some positive stroking techniques for a probation or parole officer to consider:

1. Find and reward any good performance however slight;

2. Reward frequently on a scheduled basis so that the client becomes accustomed to,and comfortable with, receiving positive strokes;

3. Shape behavior gradually, so that client needs coincide with overall probation and parole goals;

4. Use verbal and non-verbal rewards (e.g.,smile or show expressions of pleasure when a client accomplishes something desired); and

5. Develop the ability to give unconditional (spontaneous) strokes as well as conditional (earned) strokes, so that no ulterior motive or sense of bribery surfaces.

Transactional Analysis also indicates that individuals may use withdrawal, rituals, activities, pastimes, and games because of their inability to become intimate with others. A "ritual" for a PO is commonly evidenced by greeting a client in a way that reveals a lack of true concern. If the PO says, "How are you doing? How is work?", the cient may give pat answers and, as a result, meaningful communication will not be achieved.

A "pastime" for a probation or parole officer may involve simply discussing a casual interest such as professional football with clients. This might take place for an extended period before actually engaging in a serious discussion of the problems faced by them.

"Games" are different from rituals, pastimes, activities, and withdrawals, as demonstrated by their characteristics: (1) their ulterior quality, and (2) the payoff. Elements of drama and dishonesty are typically present. A person does not "come on straight" when his or her message to another person is ulterior and secret. He or she is in a sense playing a game. Robert Heise (1974) refers to a game entitled Bum Beef (or "I'm here on a bummer"). Heise states that parole violators are prime material to play this game due to their past experiences in both sending and receiving verbal communications dealing with their criminal activities. Anyone, however, is a potential candidate. The players in this game are senders or receivers. The active player is the sender and he or she is crying "bum beef." The one listening to the cry about the "bum beef" is the receiver. More than 80% of all parole violators (according to Heise) play "bum beef" for at least the first month or two after being caught. Hopefully, they are playing this game with knowledgeable receivers. The PO is usually the first receiver the violator plays this game with after being rearrested. Next, the violator or sender attempts to play this game with his or her family, friends, employer, and then anyone who listens or may be used as an agent to intervene on his or her behalf. For the violator, there is a motivation that goes deeper than that of saving face, or salvaging some kind of false pride. If he or she can win the game by convincing enough people of his or her innocence, he or she may be granted continued freedom.

Heise was previously an inmate himself and admits to observing caseworkers who become willing receivers in some of the phoniest "bum beef" games ever played. Sometimes a PO who has gone out on a limb, or taken a special interest in a client, will once again become receptive to the parolee's "bum beef" game when he or she returns.

Another area of importance in Transactional Analysis involves life scripts and decisions. Everyone has a "life script" or life plan usually formulated in his or her early years. The PO can help clients discover their life scripts and change their way of behaving by following these steps:

1. Learn to recognize the "child" within--its fears, its fun, and its abilities;

2. Recognize the parent state--its reasoning and decision making processes;

3. Recognize the child, parent, and adult states in other persons in order to promote improved social skills and interdependence;

4. Sort out the parent and child states from reality in order to foster rational behavior;and

5. Work out a system of values which is desirable and rehabilitative.

From these examples of simple yet common exchanges confronting probation and parole professionals, methods for improving the communication process and achieving tangible, significant results in probation and parole functions are outlined. The usefulness of this approach in overcoming dysfunctional responses to a variety of situations has become widely accepted and advocated in literature on the social psychology of work behavior (Eddy, 1981) and motivation theory (Lee, 1979).

Summary

With a knowledge of the elementary features of TA, and experience in their application, probation and parole officers can increase their effectiveness in supervision and management. The benefits of using TA in the work environment have proven effective in their application to private and corporate business settings, and also many areas within the public sector. Among the most important benefits derived are: (1) game avoidance; (2) effective communication; (3) improved personal relation-ships; and (4) enhanced job satisfaction.

The first benefit, game avoidance, demonstrates that games can frequently be avoided once they are recognized and remedial actions taken. By refusing to go along with another's game or to offer the expected payoff, attention can be focused more directly on the source of a client's problem and his/her most pressing needs. Similarly, the client (probationer or parolee) who attempts to engage in nonproductive or destructive games can benefit from having the negative behavior called to his/her attention and learn how to avoid future repetitions.

The second benefit, effective communication, is promoted by TA through diagnosing the ego states involved in the transactions and providing remedial measures to overcome obstacles to productive and rational communication. An awareness of actions outside the adult ego state can also serve administrators in selecting the most effective action level, considering existing constraints. If an individual is unable to engage in an adult-to-adult transaction, perhaps an adult-to-child approach is necessary. Usually, however, the achievement of an adult-to-adult transaction will render more valuable information, more rational decision-making and greater effectiveness in the communication process.

The third benefit, improved personal relationships, results primarily from the recognition and utilization of stroking techniques. Persons intent on harming themselves through negative strokes can be taught to react to positive strokes, often leading them to adopt improved self-images, overcoming their games, and recreating their life scripts. Stroking needs are usually evidenced by negative personal perceptions of one's self (or lack of self-assurance). By recognizing these underlying needs and overcoming such negative perceptions, the person is more likely to benefit in his/her future personal transactions--over which he/she will be able to exercise greater control.

A fourth benefit of increased job satisfaction is likely to evolve from an appreciation of the previous results. Probation and parole officers are called upon to deal with increasing numbers of offenders who have very complex problems. TA can help these officials better understand and more effectively cope with the perspectives and reasoning abilities of their clients, resulting in more effective treatment and integration into the mainstream of society.

BEHAVIOR MODIFICATION AND THERAPY

Behavior therapy or modification must be explained in terms of the broader concept of behavior influence (Kratcoski, 1981). Behavior influence refers to the exertion of control by one person over another and varies in magnitude. Common examples of behavior influence include public education, political campaigning, television viewing and a multitude of interpersonal interactions. Behavior modification is one form of behavior influence involving the application of experimental psychology research findings to individuals for purposes of alleviating suffering or improving behavior. It requires close monitoring and evaluation of modification efforts, and it generally attempts to improve self-control by increasing a persons' independence and analytical abilities. Behavior therapy, frequently used synonymous with behavior modification, refers more specifically to clinical intervention (i.e., therapist-patient relationship).

Proponent - B. F. Skinner

B. F. Skinner is regarded by most counseling theorists and practitioners as one of the greatest contributors to the scientific study of human behavior. He also developed a reputation as the most influential, controversial and visible American psychologist (International Encyclopedia of the Social Sciences, 1979). Skinner (1938; 1953; 1971) contributed much to the literature of behavior theory. Regarding the human condition, Skinner states:

> The struggle to avoid aversive situations is a legitimate struggle for freedom. We are certainly not beyond this. This kind of 'struggle for freedom' is mainly directed toward intentional controllers--towards those who treat others aversively in order to induce them to behave in particular ways. Thus a child may stand up to his parents, a citizen may overthrow a government, a communicant may reform a religion, a student may attack a teacher or vandalize a school, and a dropout may work to destroy a culture (Skinner, 1972, p. 27).

Principles and Application

Behavior modification techniques rely on the general principle that individuals are influenced by the consequences of their actions, and that their current environments are more relevant than other factors (e.g., early life experiences, personality characteristics) in determining their present behavior. As a result, the counselors direct their attention to observable behavior and the client's environment, rather than the client's feelings or internal processes. A frequent technique that may be used in behavior modification involves a negotiated contractual agreement (behavioral contract) with definite goals and procedures. In addition, the therapist must be able to objectively define the desired goals and to insure that they are attainable. If the client suffers from an internal crisis of identity, then another mode of treatment, such as psychotherapy, may be desired.

In the probation and parole setting, the officer must perform the role of the therapist, which may not be as difficult as one might perceive. To a large extent, the application of behavior treatment principles emphasize what is commonly regarded as "common sense," although the technique strives to add organization and structure to the process. By examining some examples of behavior therapy which can be utilized by a PO, one should be able to realize the many opportunities in which this technique may prove beneficial.

For example, if the PO smiles upon receiving the monthly report from the client and also shakes the individual's hand indicating a <u>positive</u> reaction to his/her behavior, there is a good chance the client will be more inclined to bring the report in the following month as required. This subtle form of positive reinforcement increases the probability of desirable behavior.

"Time Projection" is also a behavior modification technique. Time projections enable clients to imagine themselves functioning happily and effectively at a future date. Using this technique the client can attempt to establish productive goals which can provide guidance for his or her actions upon completion of probation or parole conditions.

Another behavior change technique is "thought control." Many clients may experience persistent and intrusive patterns of negative thoughts. Clients who experience a high degree of anxiety resulting from harmful negative thoughts may be asked to close their eyes and dwell on the destructive thoughts in the presence of the PO. The PO then voices the command, "Stop!", and draws the client's attention to the fact that the thoughts actually do stop. This is practiced several times, and the client is told to interrupt his or her own negative thoughts by mentally saying "Stop!" The client is then encouraged to practice this control technique outside the confines of the office.

The "blow-up" technique is a behavior modification technique that attempts to control or eliminate obsessional thinking. This technique requires having the client "blow-up" the distressing habit to a degree where it becomes absurd and funny. For example, a client who is afraid of stuttering because of simple nervousness would be instructed to try to stutter as much as possible. When people encourage their anticipatory anxieties to erupt, they frequently find the opposite reaction coming about. Their fears often subside and after using this method several times, the behavior they dread may eventually disappear.

The "as if" behavior therapy technique is useful for clients who complain about the negative aspects of their past life, (e.g., hostile siblings; domineering or unaffectionate parents). This procedure takes clients back in time (through concentrated thought) and allows them to fantasize in a manner which is inconsistent with their present thinking. In other words, the hostile brother would be imagined as being kind, supportive, and considerate. This experience then serves to replace directed anger with general feelings of ambivalence, serving to alleviate accumulated aggressions.

In carrying out behavior treatment, there are nine principles that a PO should remember (Lazarus, 1971):

1. He or she must decide what is solvable and what is not. This dictates what can be changed and what cannot be changed in the behavior of probationers and parolees.

2. The PO should screen out those clients for whom behavior modification or therapy is inappropriate.

3. The PO must focus on the life-role and self-esteem of the client.

4. The PO seeks out the client's reinforcers, those things which the client considers to be valuable. The PO must utilize these incentives in working out the client's treatment plan or behavior contract.

5. The PO must discover the client's behavioral expectations. Does he or she desire to change his or her behavior? Or does the individual believe he or she does not need to change?

6. The PO should specify target behaviors. Should work be done on the client's job problem or drinking problem?

7. The PO should identify the goals most beneficial to the client and the behavior necessary to achieve them.

8. The PO should shape the behavior of the client by providing constant direction and advice as the client pursues his or her goals.

9. The PO should build on success by reinforcing positive behavior.

It is possible, and frequently desirable, to apply behavior modification to more than one person. The approach may be used with a probationer's or parolee's family (Erickson, 1972). Desired behaviors in the family are also typically in need of reinforcement. For instance, families prone to problems involving alcohol can deal more effectively with an alcoholic probationer or parolee if they are taught the behavior modification technique of desensitization. Desensitization involves the process of teaching family members how to relax or to get the client to relax, when a tense situation erupts (The Workbook for Alcoholic Patients, 1975). For example, family members may be instructed in methods of focusing attention to more relaxing images (e.g., sailing), rather than immediate problems. This technique forces tempers to cool and promotes more reflective, rational reactions.

Summary

Behavior modification or therapy, in essence, is counseling which offers the probationers or parolee a new opportunity for learning more appropriate behavior. The therapy process creates a situation in which the probationer's or parolee's undesirable responses are extinguished and better responses are learned. This technique can be readily applied and successfully adapted to many of the demands of probation and parole counseling. Noted authorities in this field, however, offer the following cautionary advice which must be heeded when dealing with defendants, inmates or clients in nearly all settings (Alonzo and Braswell, 1977):

> Of course, there is no one behavioral approach which is suited to all inmates. Just as offenders bring a variety of problems to the correctional professional, so the correctional professional must also bring a variety of prevention strategies to the helping process.

Certainly, over reliance upon behavior modification therapy may be ineffective and even detrimental. Yet, as a counseling approach in the probation and parole setting, it is at times invaluable. As a result, it seems incumbent upon professionals to attempt to master, improve and expand the many techniques of behavior modification, only a few of which are explained herein.

Reality Therapy

References

Glasser, W. (1975). Reality therapy--a new approach to psychiatry. New York: Harper and Row.

Sandu, H. S. (1974). Modern corrections: The offenders, therapies, and community reintergration. Springfield, IL: Charles C. Thomas.

Selected Readings

Ackerman, J. R. (1969). Reality therapy approach to probation and parole supervision. Probation and Parole.

Blum, G. S. (1953). Psychoanalytic theories of personality. New York: McGraw-Hill.

Coleman, B. I. & Schmideberg, M. (1970). Reality therapy with offenders: Practice and principle. International Journal of Offender Therapy, 14 (1).

Evans, D. B. (1983). What are you doing? An interview with William Glasser. Personnel and Guidance Journal, 60, (8), 460-465.

Rational Emotive Therapy

References

Ellis, A. (1969). How to live with a neurotic. NY: Universal Publishing.

Ellis, A. (1974). Rational emotive psychotherapy. NY: Institute for Rational Living-Publisher.

Ellis, A. (1962). Reason and emotion in psychotherapy. NY: Lyle Stuart.

Ellis, A. (1974). The essence of rational psychotherapy: A comprehensive approach to treatment. NY: Institute for Rational Living-Publisher.

Patterson, C. H. (1973). Theories of counseling and psychotherapy. NY: Harper and Row.

Ruhnow, M. E. (1975). Supervision of group counseling. Dallas, TX: Federal Probation Office publication.

Selected Readings

Ellis, A. & Harper, R. A. (1973). A new guide to rational living. Hollywood, CA: Wilshire.

Ellis, A. (1981). Science, religiosity, and rational emotive psychology. Psychotherapy: Theory, Research, and Practice, 18 (2), 155-158.

Ellis, A. (1974). Techniques for disputing irrational beliefs. NY: Institute for Rational Living- Publisher.

Ellis, A. & Maultsby, M. C. (1974). Techniques for using rational emotive imagery. NY: Institute for Rational Living- Publisher.

Group Therapy

References

Gazda, G. M. (1971). Group counseling: A developmental approach. Boston, MA: Allyn and Bacon.

Jones, J. E., & Pfeiffer, J. W. (1975). Co-facilitating. The 1974 annual handbook for group facilitators. LaJolla, CA: University Associates Publishers.

Kelman, H. C. (1963). The role of the group in the induction of therapeutic change. International Journal of Group Psychotherapy, 13, 399-432.

Kratcoski, P. C. (1981). Correctional counseling and treatment. Belmont, CA: Duxbury Press.

Sullivan, D. F. (Ed.). (1952). Readings in group work. NY: Association Press.

Selected Readings

Beene, K. & Sheats, P.(1948). Functional roles of group members. The Journal of Social Issues, 4 (2), 42-47.

Dyer, W. G. (1969). An inventory of trainer intervention. Human Relations Training News, 41-44.

128

Frank, J. D. (1974). Some determinates, manifestations and efforts of cohesiveness in therapy groups. In G. Gazda, Basic approaches to group psychotherapy and group counseling. Springfield, IL: Charles C. Thomas.

Gendlin, E. Ground rules for group sessions, unpublished handout.

Gibb, C. A. (1954). Leadership. In Lindzeg, Handbook of social psychology. (Vol. II). Reading, MA: Addison-Wesley.

Hotfelder, P. & Sachs, A. D. (1979, June). Intake group counseling. Federal Probation.

Jones, J. E. & Pfeiffer, J. W. (1975). Styles of influence. The 1975 annual handbook for group facilitators. LaJolla, CA: University Associates Publishers.

Kemp, C. G. (1964). Perspectives on the group process. Boston, MA: The Riverside Press Cambridge Houghton Mifflin Company.

Phillips, H. (1957). Essentials of social work skills. NY: The Association Press.

Rest, W. G. & Ryan, E. J. (1970, June). Group vocational counseling for the probationer and parolee. Federal Probation.

Schwartz, W. & Zalba, S. R. (1971). The practice of group work. NY: Columbia University Press.

Wallen, J. L. (1975, February). How to recognize an effective group. Probation Officers Group Training Seminar, 134-138.

Zastowny, T. R., Janosik, E., Trimborn, S., & Milanese, E. (1982, April). Cognitive orientation, identified curative factors and depression as predictors for treatment outcomes in group therapy programs for alcoholism. Psychological Reports, 50 (2), 477-478.

Career Counseling

References

Campbell, D. P. (1974). Manual for the Strong-Campbell interest inventory. Stanford, CA: Stanford University Press.

D'Costa, A. G., Winefordner, D. W., Odgers, J. G., & Koons, P. B., Jr. (1970). Ohio vocational interest survey: Manual for interpreting. NY: Harcourt.

Department of Labor, U. S. Employment Service. (1965). Dictionary of occupational titles. (Vol. 1) Washington, DC: U. S. Government Printing Office.

Kuder, G. F. (1965). Kuder general interest survey. Chicago: Science Research Associates.

Ginzberg, E. (1972). Toward a theory of occupational choice: A restatement. Vocational Guidance Quarterly, 20, 169-176.

Selected Readings

Butcher, E. (1982). Changing by choice: A process model for group career counseling. Vocational Guidance Quarterly, 30, (3), 200-209.

Byron, W. J. (1970). Needed: A special employment clearinghouse for ex-offenders. Federal Probation.

Kelley, H. (1970). Work hard and hope for a miracle, too. Federal Probation.

Miller, J. V. (1982). Lifelong career development for disadvantaged youth and adults. Vocational Guidance Quarterly, 30, (4), 359-366.

Nakamura, S. S. (1982). An experimental focus on the development of employment for ex-offenders. Federal Probation.

Norris, W. (1972). The information service in guidance. Chicago: Rand McNally College Publishing.

U. S. Department of Labor, Bureau of Employment Security. (1965). Training and reference manual for job analysis. Washington, DC: U. S. Government Printing Office.

Psychodrama

References

Enneis, J. M. & Moreno, J. L. (1950). Hypodrama and psychodrama. Beacon, NY: Beacon House.

Gazda, G. M. (1968). Basic approaches to group
     psychotherapy and group counseling. Springfield, IL:
     Charles C. Thomas.

NiKelly, A. G. (1971). Techniques for behavior change.
     Springfield, IL: Charles C. Thomas.

Ohlsen, M. M. (1970). Group counseling. New York:
     Holt, Rinehart and Winston.

Selected Readings

Blajan-Marcus, S. (1968). Psychodrama and its diverse
     uses. International Mental Health Research
     Newsletter, 10 (2).

Buchanan, D. R. (1980). The central control model
     framework for structuring psychodramatic production.
     Group Psychotherapy, Psychodrama and Sociometry,
     33, 47-62.

Client Centered Therapy

References

Cottle, W. C., & Downie, N. M. (1960). Procedures and
     preparation for counseling. Englewood Cliffs, NJ:
     Prentice-Hall.

Kemp, C. G. (1964). Perspectives on the group process.
     Boston, MA: Houghton Mifflin Company, the Riverside
     Press.

Ohlsen, M. M. (1970). Group counseling. NY:
     Holt, Rinehard and Winston.

Patterson, C. H. (1973). Theories of counseling and
     psychotherapy. (2nd ed.). NY: Harper and Row.

Rogers, C. R. (1951). Client centered therapy. Boston,
     MA: Houghton Mifflin Company, The Riverside Press.

Shertzer, B. & Stone, S. C. (1971). Fundamentals of
     counseling. Boston, MA: Houghton Mifflin Company,
     The Riverside Press.

Yalom, I. D. (1975). The theory and practice of group
     psychotherapy. NY: Basic Books.

Selected Readings

Patterson, C. H. & Watkins, C. E. (1982). Some
    essentials of a client-centered approach to
    assessment. Measurement and Evaluation in Guidance,
    15 (1), 103-106.

Crisis Intervention

References

Cunningham, G. (1973, December). Crisis intervention in
    a probation setting. Federal Probation.

Erickson, G. D. & Hogan, T. P. (1972). Family therapy--
    an introduction to theory and technique. Monterey,
    CA: Brooks and Cole.

Harper, R. A. (1975). The new psychotherapies.
    Englewood Cliffs, NJ: Prentice-Hall.

Schwartz, J. A., Liebman, D. A., & Schwartz, C.A.
    (1975). Correctional Crisis Intervention Training
    Court.

Selected Readings

Crow, G. A. (1977). Crisis intervention. New York:
    Association Press.

Goldstein, A. P.; Minti, P. J.; Sardino, T. J.; & Green,
    D. J. (1977). Police crisis intervention.
    Kalamazoo, MI: Behaviordelia, Inc.

Hill, R. (1958). Generic features of families under
    stress. Social Casework, 39, 32-52.

Lukton, R. C. (1982). Myths and realities of crisis
    intervention. Social Casework, 63 (5), 276-285.

Pasewark, R. A., & Albers, D. A. (1972, March). Crisis
    intervention: Theory in search of a program. Social
    Work, 17, 70-77.

Reid, W. J. & Shyne, A. W. (1969). Brief and extended
    casework. New York: Columbia University Press.

Schwartz, M. C. & Weintranb, J.F. (1974, December). The
    prisoner's wife: A study in crisis. Federal
    Probation, 38, 20-26.

132

Wade, T. C., Morton, T. L., Lind, J. E., & Ferris, N. R. (1977). A family crisis intervention approach to diversion from the juvenile justice system. Juvenile Justice, 28 (3), 43-51.

Art Therapy

References

Landgarten, H. B. (1981). Clinical art therapy. New York: Branner/Mazel.

Leuner, H. (1969). Guided affective imagery (GAI). A method of intensive psychotherapy. American Journal of Psychotherapy, 23, 4-22.

Naumberg, M. (1966). Dynamically oriented art therapy: Its principle and practice. New York: Grune and Stratton.

Reyher, J. (1963). Free imagery: An uncovering procedure. Journal of Clinical Psychology, 19, 454-459.

Selected Readings

Hays, R. E. & Lyons, S. J. (1981). The bridge drawing: A projective technique for assessment in art therapy. Arts in Psychotherapy, 8 (3-4), 207-217.

Horowitz, M. (1970). Image formation and cognition. New York: Appleton-Century-Crofts.

Horowitz, M. (1963). Graphic communication: A study of interaction painting with schizophrenics. American Journal of Psychotherapy, 17, 320-327.

Kramer, E. (1965, October). Art therapy and the severely disturbed gifted child. Bulletin of Art Therapy, 3-20.

Kwiatowska, N. (1967, January). The use of families' art productions for psychiatric evaluation. Bulletin of Art Therapy, 52-69.

Naumberg, M. (1966). Psychoneurotic art: Its function in psychotherapy. NY: Grune and Stratton.

Pickford, R. (1967). Studies in psychiatric art.
    Springfield, IL: Thomas.

Pickford, R. W. (1972). Psychology and visual
    aesthetics. London, England: Anchor Press.

Transactional Analysis

References

Albano, C. (1974). Transactional analysis on the job.
    NY: AMACOM.

Berne, E. (1964). Games people play. NY: Grove Press.

Harris, T. A. (1969). I'm OK-You're OK. NY: Harper
    and Row.

Heise, R. E. (1974). Games convicts play. WA: McNeil
    Island Penitentiary.

Selected Readings

Eddy, W. B. (1981). Public organization behavior and
    development. Cambridge, MA: Winthrop.

Frazier, T. L. (1972, September). Transactional analysis
    training and treatment of staff in a correctional
    school. Federal Probation.
Huff, V. E. (1978). Creativity and transactional
    analysis. Journal of Creative Behavior, 12 (3),
    202-208.

James, M. (1975). The O.K. boss. Reading, MA:
    Addison Wesley.

James, M. (1971). Born to win. London: Addison Wesley.

Lee, R. D., Jr. (1979). Public personnel systems.
    Baltimore: University Park Press.

Nicholson, R. C. (1970, September). Transactional
    analysis: A new method for helping offenders.
    Federal Probation.

Behavior Modification and Therapy

References

Alonzo, T. M. & Brasswell, M. C. (1977, March). Behavior modification and corrections: An analysis. Lambda Alpha Epsilon: American Criminal Justice Association, 40, 10-15.

Erickson, G. D. & Hogan, T. P. (1972). Family therapy: An introduction to theory and technique. Monterey, CA: Brooks and Cole.

International encyclopedia of the social sciences. (1972). NY: Macmillan.

New Jersey Neuro-Psychiatric Institute. (1975). The workbook for alcoholic patients. Princeton, NJ: Author.

Kratcoski, P. C. (1981). Correctional counseling and treatment. Belmont, CA: Wadsworth.

Lazarus, A. A. (1971). Behavior therapy and beyond. NY: McGraw-Hill.

Skinner, B. F. (1972). Beyond freedom and dignity. NY: Bantam Books.

Skinner, B. F. (1953). Science and human behavior. NY: Macmillan.

Thorne, G. L., Tharp, R. G., & Wetzel, R. J. (1967, June). Behavior modification techniques: New tools for probation officers. Federal Probation.

Selected Readings

Bandura, A. (1962). Punishment revised. Journal of Consulting Psychology, 26, 298-301.

Gazda, G. M. (1968). Basic approaches to group psychotherapy and group counseling. Springfield, IL: Charles C. Thomas.

Harper, R. A. (1975). The new psychotherapies. Englewood Cliffs, NJ: Prentice-Hall.

Jamieson, R. B. (1965). Can conditioning principles be applied to probation? Trial Judges Journal, 4 (1).

Shah, S. (1966, June). Treatment of offenders! Some behavior principles and approaches. <u>Federal Probation</u>.

Wardlaw, G. (1981). Applied behavior analysis and crime prevention: Some cautions. <u>Australian Psychologist</u>, <u>16</u>, (3), 391-397.

Wolpe, J., Salter, A., & Reyna, L. J. (1964). <u>The conditioning therapies: The challenge in psychotherapy</u>. NY: Holt, Rinehart and Winston.

Yates, A. J. (1981). Behavior therapy: Past, present, future-imperfect? <u>Clinical Psychology Review</u>, <u>1</u> (3), 269-291.

Chapter 6

FUTURE TRENDS AND ISSUES IN
PROBATION AND PAROLE

LEARNING OBJECTIVES

*   Knowledge of nine major trends impacting probation and parole services.

*   Understanding the forces underlying future trends.

*   Recognition of major issues accompanying future trends.

*   Ability to predict future needs of probation and parole officials in accomodating change.

DISCUSSION QUESTIONS

1. Identify nine major trends impacting future probation and parole services.

2. What important issues are likely to arise from the continuance of these trends?

3. Discuss several primary factors underlying each of the future trends and the policy considerations with which probation and parole officers must be familiar.

4. Will probation and parole officials be able to accomodate each of these trends in their future delivery of services? Explain.

5. What additional issues impacting the future of probation and parole do you foresee?

138

FUTURE TRENDS AND ISSUES

While the future of probation and parole practice is by no means certain, the following selected trends should provide some indication of future issues and areas of concern to the probation and parole profession.

VICTIM COMPENSATION

According to prevailing public opinion, victims have been the forgotten persons by the criminal justice system for too long. At present there is growing interest in victim compensation programs. A recent article reports that at least 33 states have now established victim compensation programs (The (SC) State, 1982). The first state to formally institute a victim compensation program was California in 1965. Since then, at least $40 million has been paid to victims of crime nationally.

The operations of victim assistance programs differ among the states, although certain key elements are common to most. Generally, victims must file claims for any damages not covered by insurance. A governing board typically evaluates the claims and directs payment according to legislatively established guidelines. Understandably, most states have set ceilings on individual claims. For example, Maryland has a ceiling of $45,000 while Texas has a ceiling of $50,000. Most states allow limited compensation for both personal injury and property.

The role of probation and parole officers in dealing with victim compensation programs is central. An officer is likely to be asked to develop an assessment of the effects of the offender's crime upon the victim in the form of a Victim Impact Statement (VIS). Such a report is generally included in the presentence investigation report and may become crucial to the sentencing process. The following guidelines (used in the training of PO's) should illustrate the nature of VIS's and serve as a model for completing the reports:

The victim impact statement should include the following information if pertinent: first-hand statements of complainants, witnesses, and victims in relation to understanding the defendant and the offense. When applicable, include an assessment of the nature and extent of the victim's loss (i.e., victim impact statement).

This statement should contain: "information concerning any harm, including financial and social, psychological, and physical harm done to or loss suffered by any victim of the offense; and any other information that may aid the court in sentencing, including the restitution needs of the victim." Rule 32 (c), Federal Rules of Criminal Procedure, as amended by Pub. L. No. 97-291 (October 12, 1982). All parties making such statements to a probation officer should be aware that the court must disclose all such information to the defendant and the attorney for the government.

In writing a VIS, special attention should be directed to insuring clarity and conciseness, yet including all important details. The following hypothetical case illustrates a typical VIS (see Illustration 7).

ILLUSTRATION 7

VICTIM IMPACT STATEMENT

Mr. Ray Reed of Washington, D.C., was the victim of the instant offense in which the defendant hit him over the head and stole his wallet. The wallet had $50, his driver's license, credit cards, and car keys. The defendant also stole his car. The offense occurred at gun point outside Mr. Reed's apartment. Mr. Reed's 1982 Chrysler LeBaron was discovered by local police four weeks later in a damaged condition in Charlotte, North Carolina.

Although Mr. Reed was covered by insurance against loss, he was not compensated for the damage to his car by his insurance company because his car was recovered. Damages to the car included a broken windshield, two flat tires, and a smashed right front fender. Further, he had to travel to Charlotte, North Carolina, at his own expense, in order to pick up his car. Mr. Reed was also hospitalized for a slight concussion, and as a result, lost two weeks work. Mr. Reed certified by way of receipts that his total loss, because of the defendant's offense, was as follows:

Hospital bill (deductible costs): $ 100.00
Bus ticket to North Carolina: 35.00

(continued)

ILLUSTRATION 7 (continued)

Gasoline return trip:	18.50
Loss of 2 weeks work at $6.70 per hour:	536.00
Two tires at $45 each:	90.00
Windshield:	150.00
New right fender/paint job:	200.00
Cost of new driver's license:	20.00
Cash lost:	50.00
	$1,199.50

Mr. Reed also stated that he now suffers from anxiety attacks when he considers leaving his apartment at night. He would like to attend counseling for this problem but presently does not have any money for this expense. It would not be covered by his health insurance. An estimate of the cost of such counseling is $60 per session. Mr. Reed thought he might need as many as ten counseling sessions to clear up this anxiety problem.

RESTITUTION ALTERNATIVES

While the public seems to direct much of its attention and interest to the restitution of victims, citizens are also showing increased concern for additional or alternative forms of restitution. Restitution, according to recent research (Galaway, 1977), may be categorized as four separate types:

(1) MONETARY: Victim Restitution (the defendant pays the victim to compensate for his loss);

(2) MONETARY: Community Restitution (the defendant pays for a service to the community);

(3) SERVICE: Victim Restitution (the defendant performs services to help the victim);

(4) SERVICE: Community Restitution (defendant performs a useful service for the community).

For many of the same reasons which support victim compensation, community monetary restitution and compulsory services are being used more frequently as prison alternatives. An additional rationale, however, includes reimbursing governmental/community resources to alleviate increasing economic burdens. As demonstrated in the following examples, there is a growing reliance upon new forms of restitution, particularly in juvenile settings.

Restitution alternatives are especially receiving acceptance in the juvenile setting. An example of the implementation of a restitution program is typified by the provisions of one recently established in a state setting (South Carolina). This program requires juvenile offenders to repay victims for losses, damages or injuries involving either persons or property. The benefits of this program are perceived to accrue to all involved--the community, the victim and the juvenile (South Carolina Department of Youth Services, 1980). Restitution may be in the form of reparations, monetary payments or community service labors. Reparation generally involves ordering the offender to make restitution through direct service to the victim. Monetary payment typically includes reimbursing the victim through payment for the actual damages experienced. The amount of repayment is usually established by the court and may have a ceiling. If current employment opportunities are not available, the responsibility may fall upon the probation and parole officer to promote vocational training or job placement in efforts to enhance restitution possibilities. Community service alternatives are usually restricted to non-violent offenders and involve working with volunteers. An added benefit of restitution involves client development of more responsiblity and socially desirable behavior patterns. For numerous and often compelling reasons, restitution will probably continue to be emphasized in the search for alternatives to traditional incarceration practices.

COMPUTERIZATION

The "information" age has arrived in America, according to social analyst John Naisbitt (1982). The transformation from an industrial society to an information society is now underway and computer technology appears to be the focus of this transition. While courts and the criminal justice system have resisted innovation or change, increased reliance on computers is inevitable. Management information systems will become increasingly critical to probation and parole services. For instance, recent experience demonstrates the benefits of microcomputers in the supervision process. Computers can be utilized in a variety of ways, including the administration of questionnaires, psychological instruments, and educational tests. They can also provide for the analysis of family data and the completion of required reports. These benefits can free officers from many of the traditionally mundane duties and increase their time for more important supervision and treatment responsibilities.

DECENTRALIZATION

A currently felt trend in most governmental programs and agencies is one of decentralization. The movement to decentralize governmental programs has grown out of an awareness of the limitations of past centralized programs, many of which came to be perceived as failures (e.g., the national "war on poverty"). Sometimes this attitude is communicated in terms of "distrust of big government," or a "state and local government rights" approach to federalism. Within the criminal justice system, this rekindled concern for "community corrections" and decentralized services appears to have evolved for a very similar reason: the perceived ineffectiveness of centralized programs, particularly large prisons. A movement has now begun to place offenders back into community settings both for purposes of punishment and treatment.

Since PO responsibilities often center upon treatment, officers must continue to match community resources and opportunities with deserving and appropriate offenders. Past research has indicated that parolees are far more likely to be successfully reintegrated into the community if they are released from institutional environments to the care of a Community Treatment Center (CTC). The potential for success in finding employment is also greater for those re-entering the community from a local treatment center than from a traditional isolated institution (Beck, 1981). If reformation or rehabilitation is to have any chance for success, a decentralized approach to treatment seems more conducive to its attainment.

DIVERSION

Related to decentralization trends concerning increased reliance upon community corrections and treatment is the growing acceptance of pretrial diversion programs. These programs are gaining in popularity for a variety of reasons, the foremost of which is generally considered to be the financial savings over incarceration. Many, of course, will continue to be limited to offenders who are charged with non-violent types of crimes. Requirements for entry into pretrial programs are exemplified by those recently established in a state setting (South Carolina):

(1) The offender is seventeen years of age or older;

(2) There is substantial likelihood that justice will be served if the offender is placed in an intervention program;

(3) It is determined that the needs of the offender can better be met outside of the traditional criminal justice process;

(4) It is apparent that the offender poses no threat to the community;

(5) It appears that the offender is unlikely to be involved in further criminal activity;

(6) The offender is likely to respond quickly to rehabilitative treatment; and

(7) The offender has no significant history of prior delinquency or criminal activity.

With mounting concern for the structural and procedural inadequacies of the current criminal justice system in handling its workload, movement toward diversionary programs will probably continue out of necessity. It is one of the most logical directions for solutions to an already overloaded system experiencing mounting pressures.

SPECIALIZATION

In a world of increasing complexity, specialization is a trend felt by nearly all professions--the legal community, the medical profession and, certainly, the criminal justice profession. This specialization is particularly felt in the probation and parole professions. A recent indicator of this trend is a recognized emphasis on "workload" as opposed to "caseload" in super-

vision practices. The National Advisory Commission on
Criminal Justice Standards and Goals (1973) advocated the
assignment of clients on the basis of their particular
problems. For instance, clients with a specific problem
(e.g., unemployment) should be assigned to an officer
with expertise in that area of specialization (e.g., job
placement). This desire to match the special needs of a
client to a resource person with the requisite skills
should continue to evolve, especially as more time-saving
and cost-effective methods of treatment and supervision
are sought.

PREDICTION MODELS

Prediction models should continue to have a major
impact on the criminal justice system although such
models are often controversial in nature (e.g.,
predicting violence). For example, a PO officer using
the salient factor score (SFS) and guidelines developed
by the United States Parole Commission can inform a
federal judge what the average amount of time a defendant
would serve if placed in a correctional institution with
a specified sentence length. These scientifically
derived models also serve as mechanisms for guiding
judicial discretion through reliance upon acceptable
factors in considering appropriate and alternative
sentences. Past studies indicate that judges place great
importance on the probation and parole recommendations
which utilize prediction models. With the public's
increasing concern regarding the problems of sentencing
disparity and variation, it seems obvious that more
standardized methods of decision-making will eventually
become a reality.

EXPERIMENTATION AND INNOVATION

Experimentation and innovation in the delivery of
probation and parole services will inevitably increase as
the service environment continues to change. New
problems will surface and new ways for resolving them
will have to be discovered. For instance, in recent
years both nutrition and drugs have been found to have
influences on the behavior of persons with specific

psychological and physiological characteristics or ailments. In addition, new counseling and psychiatric treatment programs are proving to be successful in assisting with behavior difficulties (e.g., group counseling for job stress related disorders). As both the physical and behavioral sciences continue to study human behavior and mechanisms of control and treatment, new treatment programs will be continually tested.

Among the recent experiments that have been attempted within the probation and parole setting are the "scared straight" program (introduction to the "hardened" prison environment) and "shock probation" (temporary incarceration prior to probation). Both programs share the philosophy of insuring that an offender's first experience within the correctional environment will dissuade the individual from future criminal activity (Gatz, 1975). Preliminary results from several of these programs have been mixed, with recognition that further research is needed.

An experiment that has been attempted for improving the delivery of probation and parole within given communities is that of "satellite offices." A satellite office is one located within a community setting, rather than a courthouse. This permits a probationer or parolee to gain easier access to his or her supervising officer and improves his or her adherence to conditions of release.

Because experimentation and innovation have proven beneficial to probation and parole services, it seems certain that the need and desire for improvements will continue. Experimentation and innovation are necessary steps in resolving these demands.

ORGANIZATIONAL DEVELOPMENT AND MANAGEMENT

Probation and parole services, like the services of most public agencies, will experience new internal and external influences on both their modes of operation and the future delivery of their services. An analysis of how these influences can have an impact on the management of probation systems was the focus of a recent article by Donald Cochran (1982), a supervisor of probation services for Massachusetts. Cochran's article applies contemporary ideas and principles of organizational development to probation systems and concludes that new approaches to management are needed.

Unlike the traditional surveillance and rehabilitation orientations of most PO's, future officers will need to better understand and manage the mission and functions of their organizations. This function may involve restructuring the administration of programs whenever necessary to accomplish primary goals. It will also involve the redefinition of organizational tasks and goals. These changes will occur in an evolving environment, one which is subject to such phenomena as the cyclical baby boom, a generally declining economy, constrained resources, new political orientation, and new technologies. As a result of these trends, long term forecasting and planning capabilities will be essential.

Once management learns to appreciate and understand the forces of change upon the probation system, it will become management's duty to create an organizational climate supportive of innovation and experimentation. This climate or environment must simultaneously attempt to support principles of fairness and equity as a part of the organization's service delivery mission, and as a part of its performance accountability structure. These reforms should serve to clarify the purpose, goals and rule of the organization.

Probation and parole management will demand bold leadership and the ability to "prioritize" organizational plans. Management will have to learn to deal effectively with the problems of human motivation, applying the concepts and principles developed by modern behavioral sciences. Not only will managers need to meet these immediate internal organizational challenges, but they will also need to pursue them while experiencing considered external pressures (e.g., fiscal, demographic and correctional philosophy changes). As a result, managers will need the emotional and intellectual skills necessary for the rational and effective delivery of services in an extremely volatile environment.

Donald Cochran (1982) very succinctly summarizes the broad array of talents and strengths required of future probation and parole administrators:

> If probation is to survive and flourish, the administrators within the system are going to have to have strong technical, human relations and conceptual skills. Managers of probation systems during the 1980's are going to have to be persons of strong convictions, openmindness, courage, and a strong sense of fair play.

All of these qualities will be needed if probation managers are going to be able to establish the administrative structure that can establish a reward system, environmental climate and personnel policies that will lead to a system that will be committed to the establishment of a 'justice model' in probation, a system that believes in and supports the principles of individual rights, the dignity of man, and the resulting fair and equitable treatment of all parties concerned-- e.g., administrators, employees and clients.

References

Beck, J.L. (1981). Employment, community treatment center placement, and recidivism: A study of released federal offenders. Federal Probation, December.

Cochran, D. (1982). The 1980's. In G. Stephens (Ed.), The future of criminal justice. Cincinnati, Ohio: Anderson Publishing Company.

Eskridge, C.W. (1980). Issues in VIP management: A national synthesis. Federal Probation, September.

Galaway, B. (1977). The use of restitution. Crime and Delinquency.

Gatz, N. (1975). First shock probation: now shock parole. American Journal of Corrections, January-February, 37.

Healion, J.V. (1982, April 2). United Press International. For the victims, money won't erase the memory, but it helps. The (Columbia,SC) State.

Hurd,J.L. & Miller, K.D. (1981). Community service: What, why, and how. Federal Probation.

Naisbitt, J. (1982) Megatrends: Ten new directions transforming our lives. New York: Warner Books,Inc..

148

National Advisory Commission on Criminal Justice Standards and Goals. (1973). Report on corrections. Washington, DC: U.S. Government Printing Office.

South Carolina Department of Youth Services. (1980). Juvenile restitution: A working alternative. Columbia, SC: Author.

South Carolina Office of Pretrial Intervention. (1980) Pretrial intervention: A guide for South Carolina officers. Columbia, SC: Author.

United States Department of Justice. (1977). Federal parole guidelines. Federal Register, 42 (121), 31786.

Waldron, J., Sutton, C. and Buss, T. (1981). Professional's use of a microcomputer in a court setting. Federal Probation, December.

GLOSSARY

ALCOHOLICS ANONYMOUS. An organization founded in 1935 that assists individuals in dealing with problems of alcohol abuse.

ARRAIGNMENT. The post-indictment stage when a court considers information on defendant's alleged crimes and the defendant enters a plea to the charges.

ART THERAPY. A recently developed counseling technique used in developing trust and open communication, that involves interpreting the drawings of clients in analyzing their problems and perceptions.

BAIL. The pretrial release of a defendant by posting financial security, the amount set by a judicial official, to insure a later court appearance.

BEHAVIOR MODIFICATION AND THERAPY. Counseling treatment techniques which attempt to modify behaviors through the application of principles derived from experimental, psychological research.

BENEFIT OF CLERGY. A practice allowed in early English history that granted clerical exemption from trial and punishment to certain individuals authorized by the church.

CAREER COUNSELING. A form of counseling aimed at obtaining productive employment and desired career goals for clients with occupational needs.

CLIENT CENTERED THERAPY. An approach in counseling that is based upon the cultivation of a close and trusting relationship between counselor and client that promotes self-actualization and psychological adjustment to problems.

CLIENT MANAGEMENT CLASSIFICATION (CMC). An innovative approach to classifying and managing adult probation and parole clients by the designated authority, through rapid needs assessment and appropriate case-work planning.

COMMUNITY CORRECTIONS. Conditions, sentences or programs involving the placement of offenders in the community rather than incarceration.

CONCURRENT SENTENCE. A criminal sentence that is not compounded on, or added to an existing sentence, but instead "runs" concurrently with it.

CONSECUTIVE SENTENCES. Sentences that are added together in determining the total time to be served.

CRISIS INTERVENTION. The devlopment of approaches for defusing hostile dispute situations encountered in client supervision by applying techniques for restoring order and resolving conflicts.

DEFENDANT. A person against whom an action is brought in a criminal case by the state (or federal government) for an alleged criminal violation.

DETERRENCE. Punishment aimed at preventing future criminal behavior, both specifically (e.g., the person imprisoned), and generally (e.g., the population aware of the consequences).

DIVERSION. An administrative procedure which permits selected offenders to bypass formal adversary proceedings by participating in a treatment-oriented program, thus avoiding a formal conviction.

FINE. A sum of money adjudged payable by the defendant to a public treasury, as a form of punishment for the commission of a crime.

GROUP COUNSELING. An experience based model of counseling that relies upon group processes for a framework of problem-solving and human learning.

HALFWAY HOUSE. A place of residence for formerly institutionalized offenders that is designed to facilitate their readjustment to private life.

INCAPACITATION. Incarceration for purposes of physically restraining offenders and preventing further criminal behavior.

INMATE. A person confined in a penal institution.

JUDICIAL REPRIEVE. An early English practice that permitted a delay or suspension of punishment by the court when considered appropriate.

JURISDICTION. The legal authority of a court to hear and decide a case.

MISDEMEANOR. An offense that is less serious than a felony and generally has a less severe penalty.

NOLLE PROSEQUI (or NOL. PROS.). A decision by a prosecutor not to prosecute or proceed with an alleged criminal case.

NOLO CONTENDERE. The Latin term meaning "no contest," which is an infrequent plea that normally has the immediate consequence of a guilty plea, but may benefit the defendant in subsequent civil actions or lessen the social stigma associated with confessed guilt.

PAROLE. The conditional release to the community of a prisoner prior to completion of the original sentence by a parole board.

PAROLE BOARD. An official body which determines whether inmates will be released from incarceration to the community prior to completion of criminal sentences.

PLEA BARGAINING. An agreement entered into by a prosecutor and a defendant whereby concessions are generally made, e.g., reduced charges or sentences, in return for a guilty plea.

PRESENTENCE INVESTIGATION. An investigation by a probation officer that serves as a basis for a formal report given to the court to assist in sentencing.

PRETRIAL RELEASE. A process that permits a defendant to be released to the community prior to trial, and sometimes in lieu of trial.

PRIOR RECORD. The criminal history of an individual frequently reviewed in presentence investigations and considered in the sentencing process.

PROBATION. A sentence given to a convicted offender which is to be served in the community without incarceration, under conditions of supervision by probation officers.

PROSECUTOR. An attorney representing the government with the responsibility of initiating and pursuing criminal proceedings against accused criminals.

PSYCHODRAMA. A counseling technique involving the reenactment of life situations which reveals personal difficulties through role portrayals, and leads to improved self-understanding and reorientation.

RATIONAL EMOTIVE PSYCHOTHERAPY. A therapy which assumes that many disturbing behaviors result from irrational thinking which can be converted to rational thinking through reorganizing perceptions and promoting logical self-verbalizations.

REALITY THERAPY. A modern counseling approach which assists individuals to accept reality and gain self-respect through greater involvement with others.

RECIDIVISM. A return to criminal behavior.

RECOGNIZANCE (RELEASE ON OWN RECOGNIZANCE). An obligation in a court of law to perform a specified duty, e.g., to appear in court, as a condition for release.

REFERRAL. A process used by probation and parole authorities in arranging appropriate treatment and assistance programs beyond their agencies for probation and parole clients.

REHABILITATION. An approach to punishment which attempts to change the offender's criminal behavior through appropriate treatment.

RESTITUTION. A sentencing alternative that requires an offender to compensate a victim or society for the damage incurred by the offender's crime.

RETRIBUTION. A philosophy that punishment should fit the crime, and that society is morally justified in exacting proportionate penalties for wrongdoing.

REVOCATION. An action taken by the court or the parole authority which removes a person from probation or parole, because of a violation of conditions of release.

RISK PREDICTION SCALE. A device used by probation or parole authorities to determine the appropriate level of client supervision.

SALIENT FACTOR SCORE. A measurement device that is part of a statistically based instrument for predicting and recommending the length and severity of sentences.

SHOCK PROBATION. A punishment technique that requires an offender to serve a short prison term prior to release on probation for purposes of encouraging future crime avoidance and behavior changes.

STARE DECISIS. A Latin word meaning "let the decision stand," which is used as a rule for applying precedents in legal reasoning.

SUSPENDED SENTENCE. A process whereby the court delays or stays the execution of a sentence and usually imposes conditions of probation.

TICKET-OF-LEAVE. An historic conditioned release of an offender that was granted for good behavior and revoked for misconduct.

TRANSACTIONAL ANALYSIS. A counseling theory aimed at improving interpersonal relationships by focusing on three primary ego states (parent, adult, child) which are used in analyzing human transactions and behaviors.

VICTIM IMPACT STATEMENT. A report typically used in presentence investigations which assesses the impact of a crime on the victim.

VOLUNTEER. A possible alternative resource for probation and parole systems which involves using non-paid staff to assist in performing various office responsibilities.

WORK RELEASE (or FURLOUGH). A program that permits an inmate to be conditionally released to the community prior to sentence completion for purposes of engaging in productive employment.

INDEX

EXERCISE 1

The Presentence Investigation (PSI) Report

Instructions: Prior to completion of this exercise, the
student   should   review   the   discussion   of   presentence
investigation contained in Chapter IV.   Having completed
the review, the following hypothetical presentence report
worksheet   and   final   presentence   report   is   to   be   read
thoroughly by the student.   The hypothetical reports are
based on information that is typical of that required   in
the probation setting.   The reports are designed from the
actual   forms used in the U.S.   Federal Probation System.
The proper completion of the reports is one of the   major
responsibilities   of   the   PO,   and serves as an   important
factor   in the final sentencing of the   defendant.   Now,
using   the   information   below   (along   with   additional
information),   complete   the blank PSI worksheet   in   its
entirety.   Following its completion (at the discretion of
the   course   instructor) use this information as a   basis
for a final PSI report,   similar to the one performed   on
Joe Doe (hypothetical defendant).   Be sure to recommend a
final   sentence   for   the   defendant.   Clarity   and
conciseness   are   of   tremendous   significance,   as   these
reports   are   generally reviewed by the   Chief   Probation
Officer,   and finally the presiding judge.   For the items
of   information   not   provided,   use   information   about
yourself,   or   hypothetical   information,   as   required.
Reasonable and creative thoughts are encouraged.   Be sure
to leave no item unanswered.

Hypothetical   Facts: The   defendant   is   charged   with   a
violation   of 21 USC 844A (Possession of Marijuana   - 1st
Offense;   maximum   sentence: 1 year/$1000   fine).   The
defendant was arrested on September 1, 198__ and released
on   a personal recognizance bond the following day.   The
defendant   advises defense   counsel,   J.   Lee   Baity,   to
notify the Assistant U.S.   Attorney,   I.   Gotchew, that a
plea of guilty is desired.

PROB 1 (Rev. 11/78)	UNITED STATES DISTRICT COURT	DISTRICT	DOCKET NUMBER
	Federal Probation System	of Mass.	77-00124-01
	WORKSHEET FOR PRESENTENCE REPORT	SENTENCING JUDGE	SENTENCING DATE
	(See Publication 105 for Instructions)	Montgomery	Oct. 14, 1977

1. IDENTIFYING DATA

COURT NAME (Last, first, middle) AKA	DATE OF FIRST INTERVIEW
Doe, John	Oct. 1977
	REPORT DUE
	as assigned
TRUE NAME (Last, first, middle)	RECORDED BY
	probation officer

CURRENT ADDRESS (Directions, how long)	LEGAL ADDRESS (if different)	CONSENT FORMS SIGNED
		☒ YES ☐ NO
Hampden County House of	71 Lee Avenue	RACE
Corrections	Holyoke, Mass.	Caucasian
		CITIZENSHIP
		U.S.

PHONE NO.	AGE	BIRTHDATE	BIRTHPLACE	SEX	MARITAL STATUS
782-4003	28	11-15-48	Boston, Mass.	M	Divorced

NO. OF DEPENDENTS	SOC. SEC. NO.	FBI NO.	OTHER IDENTIFYING NO.
one (child)	987-65-4321	999 888 H	

2. OFFENSE

OFFENSE AND DATE OCCURRED	DATE, BY WHOM AND WHERE ARRESTED
Viol. Title 21; USC, 841(A)(1) & 846 (Cowsp. & Dist. of Heroin)	

PLEA OR VERDICT	CUSTODIAL STATUS
Guilty to Mass. Indict. on 9-29-77 Will plead guilty under rule 20 to w/d tx. Indict.	IN CUSTODY IN LIEU OF $100,000 SURETY BOND SINCE 8-15-77

PENALTY

Imprisonment 15 yrs./$25,000 & special parole term (SPT) of at least 3 yrs.(each count)

ASST. U.S. ATTORNEY	DEFENSE COUNSEL (Name, address, & phone no.)
	Richard Pratt ☐ APPOINTED ☒ RETAINED
David Crawford	981 Maine St., Springfield, MA

3. DEFENDANT'S VERSION (Summary of offense and arrest by defendant/explanation and reasons for involvement)

Defendant going to Mexico on vacation along with co-defendant, Nancy Rooney. A guy she met wanted some heroin. He shows up in El Paso and demands to know where the stuff is. Nancy agreed to get him some and asked the defendant to come along. Defendant states he was there so he guesses he is guilty. Defendant arrested by Mexican police but released him. States he doesn't deserve to go to jail.

4. OTHER DEFENDANT INFORMATION (Relative culpability of all the defendants)

Co-defendant, Nancy Rooney, in custody in Mexico awaiting trial.

5. PRIOR RECORD (List below all other arrests whether convicted or not including juvenile adjudication)

DATE Juvenile	AGE	OFFENSE	REASON FOR INVOLVEMENT	COURT OF CONVICTION	DISPOSITION	COUNSEL YES	NO	WAIVED
11-5-62	14	Using motor veh. w/o authority	joy riding	Springfield, Juvenile Crt.	1 yr. probation	x		
10-28-63	15	Break. & Entering	broke in private resi.	Holyoke, Dist. Ct.	committed, youth service board	x		
12-23-68	20	shoplifting	stealing jewl. in dept. store	Springf. PD	dismissed			
5-11-69	20	rec. stolen property	stolen TV set from pawn shop	Holyoke Dist. Ct.	4 mos. county suspen. prob. 2 yrs.	x		
9-15-70	21	burglary & enter. in nighttime	arrested inside drug store-nite	Northhampton/ Dist. Ct./	6 mos. county jail	x		
6-27-75	25	larceny over $100 & forgery	withdrew $500 w/forged withd.	Hampden /Co. Superior Ct./	2 yrs. S.S.; 18 mo. prob. w/rgst.	x		

6. ADDITIONAL DATA (Detainers or charges pending; previous probation/parole and institutional history, dates, report of adjustment, present release status)

Rule 20, w/d of Texas--same offense as

6. PERSONAL AND FAMILY DATA (If essential, include home and neighborhood, religion, previous addresses, interests and use of leisure time)

Parents--natives of Austria. Violent arguments between parents. Wife thinks husband drinks excessively. Police called due to domestic quarrels (no arrests). Mrs. Doe had TB (1955). Children placed in West. Mass home until Mrs. Doe recovered. Defendant remained home.

160

6. Cont. NAMES OF IMMEDIATE FAMILY (List spouse & children under item 7. MARITAL)

NAME	RELATIONSHIP	AGE	PRESENT ADDRESS	OCCUPATIONAL	PRIOR RECORD YES	PRIOR RECORD NO
Henry Doe	Father	59	Holyoke, MASS	machine opera.		x
Geraldine Ericksen Doe	Mother	58	" "	housewife		x
Stanley Doe	Brother	24	" "	unemployed		x
Audrey Doe	Sister	19	" "	college stud.		x

7. MARITAL (Present and previous marriages, including cohabitation)

NAME OF SPOUSE	AGE	PLACE AND DATE OF MARRIAGE	No. of Children	Outcome of Marriage
Barbara Raymond	20	Hartford, Conn., Nov. 22, 1968	1	Divorced 12/28/71
Pregnant at time of marriage				

NAMES OF CHILDREN (Including those from previous marriages)	AGE	ADDRESS, SCHOOL, CUSTODY, SUPPORT
John	8	custody of mother (attends public school)

ATTITUDE OF SPOUSE AND CHILDREN TOWARD DEFENDANT AND HOME ATMOSPHERE

defendant required to pay $20 weekly child support

8. EDUCATION

HIGHEST GRADE COMPLETED	AGE LEFT SCHOOL	REASON FOR LEAVING
10th	17	older than classmates and wanted to get a job

OTHER TRAINING RECEIVED (Business or trade)

NAME OF SCHOOL (List schools attended; start with last school)	LOCATION	ATTENDED FROM/TO	DEGREE RECEIVED
Baram H. S.	Holyoke, Mass.	fall '64	Nov. '65

SUMMARY OF SCHOOL DATA (Test Results, Academic Rating, Class Standing, Behavior)

9. EMPLOYMENT (Cover last ten years including reasons for periods of unemployment or disability)

DATES	NAME AND ADDRESS OF EMPLOYER	NATURE OF WORK, WEEKLY WAGE, REASON FOR LEAVING
STARTED Nov. 76 ENDED present	Unemployed, collected unemployment comp. $72.00 weekly	
STARTED Aug. 74 ENDED Nov. 76	Smith Chemical Co. Northhampton, MASS.	forklift operator $4.10/hr.
STARTED March 72 ENDED Dec. 73	United Rug Co. Easthampton	Warehouse $2.75/hr. quit due to disagreement over hours
STARTED 1968 ENDED 1971	Roofing business	(3-4 mos. in any year)
STARTED Apr. 66 ENDED Oct. 68	Central Bakery, Inc. Holyoke, MASS.	worked on delivery truck - minimum wage lost job when co. went out of business
STARTED ENDED		
STARTED ENDED		

OCCUPATIONAL SKILLS, INTERESTS, AND AMBITIONS

Page 4

162

10. HEALTH

PHYSICAL DESCRIPTION (Height, weight, scars, illnesses being treated; health problems, and all past and present treatment and medication)

Good physical conditions

DRUG ABUSE, ALCOHOL, NARCOTICS (Age use began, frequency/cost, type of drug, past and present treatment)

Denial use of narcotics
Urinalysis negative

MENTAL AND EMOTIONAL (Self evaluation, personality traits, disorders, treatment)

I.Q. 102   113

Youth Services Board (1963)

Court Ordered Examination

11. MILITARY SERVICE

SERVICE NUMBER	BRANCH OF SERVICE	DATE OF ENTRY	DATE DISCHARGED	TYPE OF DISCHARGE
HIGHEST RANK HELD	RANK AT SEPARATION	DECORATIONS AND AWARDS		VA CLAIM NUMBER

SUMMARY OF MILITARY DATA

12. FINANCIAL CONDITION

LIST FINANCIAL ASSETS (Real estate, insurance, real and personal property, stocks, bonds, checking and saving accounts, income from pensions and compensation, rentals, and family income, net worth, ability to pay fine or restitution)	LIST FINANCIAL LIABILITIES (INCLUDING BALANCE DUE AND MONTHLY PAYMENTS FOR home mortgage, rent, utilities, medical, personal property, home repairs, charge accounts, loans, taxes, fines, restitution, pending civil suits)

<u>Confiscated</u>
 	
'77 Cadillac $10,640
 Speedboat w/motor $4,000
 	
Mother w defendant's savings acc't.
   $7,146.23
   questions surrounding this money
	GMAC (loan) for Cadillac $4,200
	                    (balance)
	
	(Defendant plans to make no further
	 payments unless car is returned)

13. EVALUATION (the probation officer's professional assessment of the defendant)

14. SENTENCING DATA (Use appropriate forms and charts)

15. ALTERNATIVE PLANS (Provide a statement of realistic sentencing alternatives available to the court and treatment plan)

164

UNITED STATES DISTRICT COURT

PRESENTENCE REPORT

NAME (Last, First, Middle) Doe, John Q.		DATE October 14, 1977
ADDRESS Hampden County House of Correction	LEGAL ADDRESS 71 Lee Avenue Holyoke, Mass.	DOCKET NO. 77-00124-01 RACE Caucasian CITIZENSHIP U.S.

AGE 28	DATE OF BIRTH 11-15-48	PLACE OF BIRTH Boston, Mass.	SEX Male	EDUCATION 10th grade

MARITAL STATUS Divorced	DEPENDENTS One, in custody of former wife	
SOC. SEC. NO. 987-65-4321	FBI NO. 999 888 H	OTHER IDENTIFYING NO.

OFFENSE

   D/Mass.--Consp. & Dist. heroin, 21:USC, 841(a) (1) & 846

PENALTY

   0-15 years and/or $25,000 and SPT of at least 3 yrs. on each count

CUSTODIAL STATUS

   In custody in lieu of $100,000 surety bond since 8-15-77

PLEA

   Guilty to Mass. Ind. 9-29-77; will plead under Rule 20 to W/D Tx. Ind.

VERDICT

DETAINERS OR CHARGES PENDING
   Rule 20, W/D Tx, Doc. #77-00135-01, Violation of 21:USC, 952 (a) & 960 (a) (1) &
841(a) (1), same penalty.

OTHER DEFENDANTS
   Nancy Rooney, in local custody in Mexico

ASSISTANT U.S. ATTORNEY
  David Crawford, Esq.
	DEFENSE COUNSEL
	  Philip Pratt, Esq.
	  981 Main Street
	  Springfield, Mass. (413) 555-4321 (Retained)

DISPOSITION

SENTENCING JUDGE	DATE

PRESENTENCE REPORT

OFFENSE

Official Version.   John doe is the subject of two
separate indictments, one in the District of
Massachusetts and one in the Western District of Texas.
On August 20, 1977, the Grand Jury in Massachusetts
returned an indictment against Doe and Nancy Rooney
charging that they conspired between May 28, 1977, and
July 30, 1977, to distribute a quantity of heroin and
that they distributed that heroin on June 23, 1977.

On August 26, 1977, a grand jury in El Paso, Texas,
returned an indictment against Doe and Rooney charging
that they imported 101.7 grams of heroin into the United
States on or about July 30, 1977, and that they
distributed that heroin on the same date at El Paso,
Texas.   Doe appeared on September 29, 1977, and pled
guilty to the Massachusetts indictment. He has indicated
his intention to plead guilty to the Texas indictment
under Rule 20.

This investigation began in May 1977 when the Drug
Enforcement Agency received information that Doe was
looking for a buyer for a large quantity of heroin.   On
May 28, 1977, an undercover agent was introduced to Doe
at a bar in Springfield and Doe acknowledged that he was
looking for a buyer for a kilo of heroin.   He was
initially reluctant to deal with a stranger but, after
four meetings, he offered to make the agent a partner if
the agent agreed to purchase the heroin as soon as it
came across the border into Texas.   The agent accepted
the offer but insisted on first receiving a sample of the
heroin.

On June 23, 1977, the agent and Doe met in Springfield
and drove to a shopping mall where they met Doe's
girlfriend, Nancy Rooney.   After receiving instructions
from Doe, Rooney went to her car and returned with a
sample of 2.70 grams of heroin which she gave to the
agent.   The latter paid Doe $300.   The substance was
tested and found to contain 31.7 percent heroin.

On July 21, 1977, the agent informed Doe that the sample
was of acceptable quality.   On July 24, Doe instructed
the agent to meet him in El Paso, Texas, on July 29.   The
agent flew to El Paso where he met with Doe and Nancy
Rooney at the Yellow Rose Hotel.   At 8:15 a.m., on July
30, Doe and Rooney crossed the border into Juarez.   They
returned two hours later and Doe told the agent that he

was able to obtain only a quarter kilogram of heroin.
The agent expressed disappointment but Doe said that the
heroin was of very high quality and could be cut many
times. Doe then sold the agent the first installment of
101.7 grams for $4,000. Tests determined that this
substance contained 44.6 percent heroin. Doe explained
that he and Rooney would return to Mexico that afternoon
to obtain the balance.

Doe and Rooney crossed into Juarez and were arrested by
Mexican police later in the day. Nancy Rooney had 147.3
grams of heroin in her possession. No heroin was found
on Doe who was released after two days in custody.
Rooney was held for trial. Doe returned to Massachusetts
where he was arrested on August 14, 1977.

<u>Defendant's Version</u>. "I was going to Mexico on a
vacation and Nancy decided to come with me. This guy she
met in Springfield was pestering her to get him some
heroin. I had seen him a couple of times in June. All
of a sudden he shows up in El Paso and demands to know
where the stuff is. She finally agreed to get him some
and she asked me to come in case anything happened. I
was there so I guess I'm guilty. All of a sudden I was
arrested by the Mexican cops but they let me go because
they didn't have anything on me. Then, all of a sudden
I'm arrested up here. My lawyer says entrapment is hard
to prove so I guess I'm guilty. But I didn't say all
those things the narc claims. I don't deserve to go to
jail.

PRIOR RECORD

<u>Juvenile Adjudications</u>

11-05-62   Using motor vehicle Springfield, Mass. 1 year
Age 14   without authority   Juvenile Court   probation

Mr. Doe was represented by counsel. He and two other
juveniles stole a car and went on a "joy ride." Mr. Doe
made a good adjustment on probation during the initial
months, but became increasingly uncooperative thereafter.

10-28-63   Breaking & Entering Holyoke   Committed, Youth
Age 15   District   Service Board
                                   Court

Mr. Doe was represented by counsel. He and one other
juvenile broke into a home in Holyoke. The Youth Service
Board sent him to the Industrial School at Shirley,
Massachusetts, where he remained until June 1964 when he

was paroled. he was discharged one year later. His institutional performance was routine. He participated in a woodworking course and was placed on report on one occasion for fighting in the dining hall.

Adult Record

12-23-68   Shoplifting   Springfield   Dismissed, lack
Age 20   of prosecution

Doe was arrested after he allegedly attempted to steal several jewelry items from a department store. The store manager declined to press charges.

9-15-70   Burglary & Entering   Northhampton   6 mos. County
Age 21   in the nighttime   District Ct.   Jail

Mr. Doe was represented by counsel. He was apprehended at 2:15 a.m., inside a drug store. He had activated a silent alarm when he entered the building. Jail officials recall that Mr. Doe attempted to be reclusive while incarcerated. He voluntarily spent several months in segregation because of his fear of attack by other inmates.

6-27-75   Larceny over   Hampden Cty.   2 yrs. prison ss;
Age 25 $100 and   Superior Ct.   18 mos. prob. w/
          Forgery   restitution

Mr. Doe was represented by counsel. He withdrew $500 from a bank account using a stolen passbook and forged withdrawal slips. He was identified through bank photographs. Mr. Doe paid $310 in restitution and the balance was remitted. He performed well under probation supervision.

PERSONAL AND FAMILY DATA

Defendant. John Doe ws born on October 15, 1948, in Boston, Massachusetts. His parents, natives of Austria, came to the United States as displaced persons after World War II. The family has lived for the last fifteen years at their present residence in Holyoke. The defendant's early years were turbulent because of many violent arguments between his parents. These were caused by Mrs. Doe's belief that her husband was an excessive drinker. She summoned police assistance on several occasions although no arrests were made. In 1955 Mrs. Doe contracted tuberculosis. She was hospitalized for almost one year and the father was unable to keep the family together. The defendant and his siblings were placed in the Western Massachusetts Home for Children but the family was reunited when Mrs. Doe recovered. The defendant remained with his family until he married at the age of twenty. He returned to the family home after his divorce three years later.

Mr. and Mrs. Doe picture their son as a well-intentioned individual whose difficulties with the law were caused by his unwise selection of associates. They are bitter towards codefendant Nancy Rooney whom they believe was responsible for this offense. They view his previous juvenile and adult transgressions as minor matters which were treated with undue harshness by police and the courts. His parents describe the defendant as an intelligent and ambitious individual who values financial success above all else. They are proud of the fact that, in recent years, the defendant has acquired such material possessions as an expensive automobile and a boat. They also note that he has been especially generous with his younger brother and sister.

Parents and Siblings. The father, Henry Doe, age 59, resides with his family and for the last seventeen years has been employed as a machine operator earning a moderate salary. The home atmosphere improved considerably when Mr. Doe stopped drinking approximately five years ago. The mother, Geraldine Ericksen Doe, age 58, resides with her husband and is a housewife. Her health is poor due to respiratory ailments.

There are two siblings. Stanley Doe, age 24, resides with his parents and is unemployed. Stanley believes that his brother is the victim of harassment by law enforcement authorities. Audrey Doe, age 19, resides with her parents and is a community college student.

Marital. John Doe married Barbara Raymond in a civil ceremony in Hartford, Connecticut on November 22, 1968. Both parties were 20 years old at the time and she was pregnant. The couple had one child, John Jr., who was born on April 29, 1969. Mrs. Doe reports the the marriage was troubled from the start by financial problems since the defendant was unemployed. He turned to illegal means of supporting the family and his subsequent arrests caused even more strain on the couple's relationship. There were several brief separations during 1969 and 1970, and in September of 1970. When he was released, Mrs. Doe found him a "different man" and it was impossible to reconstitute their relationship. The Hampden County Probate Court granted a divorce on December 28, 1971, on grounds of incompatibility and awarded her custody of the child. The defendant was required to pay $20 a week child support. Mrs. Doe is employed as a telephone operator. She reports that her ex-husband's support payments have been sporadic. He often goes for months without visiting the child or making any payments but he will then arrive with lavish gifts for his son and lump sum support payments. Mrs. Doe says that her relationship with the defendant is now amicable but they see each other infrequently.

Mr. Doe asserts that he has no plans to marry again. He stated that Nancy Rooney was merely a friend.

Education. Mr. Doe was educated in local public schools. He left junior high school in October 1963 when he was committed to the Youth Service Board. He returned to Baran High School in Holyoke in the fall of 1964 and dropped out of the eleventh grade in November 1965.

School officials describe Mr. Doe as an intelligent individual who never worked up to his capabilities. His grades were generally C's and D's. Mr. Doe left school because he was older than most of his classmates, and wanted to get a job.

Employment. Between November 1976 and the time of his arrest Mr. Doe was unemployed and collected unemployment compensation of $72 a week. From August 1974 to November 1976, he was a forklift operator at the Smith Chemical Company in Northhampton. He earned $4.10 an hour but he was subject to frequent layoffs. Company officials described him as an uncooperative employee with a high degree of tardiness. He would not be considered for reemployment.

Between March 1972 and December 1973, Mr. Doe worked in the warehouse of the United Rug Company in Easthampton, Massachusetts. He earned $2.75 an hour and he quit after a disagreement over hours. Between 1968 and 1971, Mr. Doe was sporadically employed in the roofing business. This work paid well but he seldom was able to get more than 3 or 4 months work in any year.

After he left high school, Mr. Doe worked on a delivery truck for Central Bakery, Inc., of Holyoke. He held this job between Aril 1966 and October 1968 and earned the minimum wage. He lost this job when the company went out of business.

Mr. Doe said that he would like someday to open his own business. He had no clear ideas about the nature of this business but stressed that he saw himself in a managerial capacity and would hire others to do the menial labor.

HEALTH

Physical. Mr. Doe is in good physical condition. He denies having used drugs of any kind and he specifically disclaims the use of heroin. Discussion with family members as well as with law enforcement sources revealed no information that would contradict Mr. Doe's assertions in this respect. A physical examination and urinalysis test performed at the jail were negative for heroin use.

Mental and Emotional. On two occasions Mr. Doe was tested in public schools and received I.Q. scores of 102 and 113.

Mr. Doe has been examined by mental health professionals on two occasions. The first occurred shortly after Mr. Doe was committed to the Youth Service Board in 1963. A psychologist diagnosed him as, "a person whose anxiety is stimulated by a frustrated need for affection. Herman has developed no healthy conscience. His response to social demands is not based on an close commitment to moral principles."

Mr. Doe was examined once again as a result of this court's pretrial order. Dr. Robert Land administered a battery of psychological tests, the results of which suggested, "that he seems to be unusually fearful of being overpowered and destroyed. It is obvious that he has been unable to resolve childhood problems and continues to feel quite rejected. He tends to view threatening environmental forces as coming outside his control."

FINANCIAL CONDITION

Assets. Mr. Doe lists two main assets: one is a 1977 Cadillac purchased in January of that year for $10,640. This automobile was confiscated by the Drug Enforcement Administration. The other asset is a 19-foot fiberglass speedboat with a 115 horsepower Mercury outboard engine worth approximately $4,000.

Mr. Doe's parents displayed to the probation officer a savings account passbook with a present balance of $7,146.23. The account was listed to Mr. Doe and his mother, but the parents made it clear that the defendant had made the deposits. When questioned about this, Mr. Doe asserted that the account in fact belonged to his mother and that his name was on it only as a matter of convenience. His mother subsequently contacted the probation officer and retracted her earlier statement. She said that she made a mistake and that the money in the account belonged to her.

Liabilities. The only debt Mr. Doe lists is a loan from GMAC to finance the purchase of his 1977 Cadillac. The loan balance is presently $4,200 and Mr. Doe plans to make no further payments until such time as his car is returned to him by the Government.

EVALUATION

Although he attempts to shift responsibility to his codefendant, Mr. Doe was the principal figure in the importation and sale of over 100 grams of high quality heroin. Were it not for the intervention of the Mexican authorities, he would have completed the sale of a quarter kilogram to an undercover agent. Mr. Doe is not a user of the drug. He apparently values financial success to the point that he made a calculated decision that heroin trafficking was profitable. His lack of concern about the moral aspects of his decision confirms the observation of mental health professionals that his personality lacks some of the constraints under which most people operate. For Mr. Doe, participation in this offense, as well as in earlier offenses, was a logical means of satisfying his economic motives.

The members of Mr. Doe's family are intensely loyal to him and they have an unrealistic view of his participation in criminal activities. They do not question the sources of his assets, which are surprisingly large for a person with his employment history. The family cannot be counted upon to exert the pressure that might convince Mr. Doe to conform to law abiding behavior. Mr. Doe himself is unrealistic in his personal goals. Without much education or skill, he expects a high degree of financial compensation, but he has not thus far shown a willingness to work towards that goal. It is unlikely that Mr. Doe will attempt conventional paths to economic success until he is convinced that illegal means are too hazardous.

172

RECOMMENDATION

The probation office recommends commitment to the custody of the Attorney General and a mandatory special parole term of three years. This recommendation considers the quanitity and quality of the heroin involved, and the defendant's prior record.

The court may wish to consider imposing sentence under 18 U.S.C. 4205(b) (2) so that the Parole Commission can release him in the event that institutional conditions present a critical hazard to his mental health. The court might also consider recommending commitment to a minimum security institution where Mr. Doe would feel less threatened.

Respectfully submitted,

Matilda Gormally
U.S. Probation Officer

Approved: _____
J. Grant Hogan
Chief U.S. Probation Officer